Dorothy Squires Tortured Diva

A Personal Memoir By Her Friend & Confidant

David Bret

A catalogue record for this book is available from the British Library.

ISBN: 978-1539948599

Contents

Introduction

In a November 1972 press-statement, Dorothy Squires told her fans, "When I walk out on stage at the Palladium, I wish you could stand where I stand—your welcoming cheers and your love, and the warmth that envelops me almost makes my heart burst with pride. Thank you for making it all worthwhile."

Dot's concerts were "happenings" like nothing before or since in British show business history, making her perhaps the only *chanteuse-réaliste* we ever had and quite possibly the finest British female singer of the last century. The undiluted emotion of a Squires performance had to be experienced to be believed—the feeling of elation almost indescribable. Once Dot entered your heart, she stayed there and for that one evening there was precious little room for anyone or anything else. Her fans and friends were obliged to share her triumphs and tragedies, her joys and sorrows, though essentially she was a very private person.

I never visited Dot's home. We met or talked on the phone—when she was not working this would be twice weekly, though there were times when we would not talk for weeks, and she would bawl, "Where the *fuck* have you been?"

Dot could out-curse a sailor on shore leave, yet coming from her those expletives were *so* funny. Sometimes after her concerts we—by "we" I mean my wife, Doris or Brenda (her secretaries), her saxophonist Johnnie Gray, her straight-talking orchestra leader Nicky Welsh, and a few hangers-on—would retreat to the theatre bar or a local pub or club to sit in the shadows and "chew the fat". If we were within fifty miles of her home and Matt, her chauffeur, had been given the night off, there would be "car chats" with just Dot, Jeanne and myself—Dot and Jeanne leaning or sitting on the bonnet of her car and me sitting cross-legged on the roof! Dot told me things about herself and some of those who had "wafted" into her life that I would never repeat to a living soul. We laughed, we cried, swapped dirty jokes, and made fun of people we disliked.

She once told me, "In public I have always tried to present myself as calm and confident, even though I've been burning away inside. Misery and solitude are personal emotions which should never be inflicted on other people. I always cry in private."

Dot could be her own worst enemy: sublimely talented, during the latter years of her career she took all those slings and arrows—there were many—to heart, instead of letting them bounce off the steely hide she claimed to have. I was her friend and confidant for over twenty years—towards the end of her life, for a little while, we lived just a few miles apart. I witnessed her at her highest when she was one of Britain's most feted entertainers, hiring concert halls up and down the country—including the London Palladium—and performing to raucous, sell-out audiences. I was also there to share her sorrows when her career was on the wane and she had sunk to the very depths of despair and had to rely on the charity of friends in order to survive because her family wanted nothing to do with her, or she them.

"Like most families when one member does well, they only cared about me when they wanted something," she said.

Astonishingly, this is the first ever biography of Dorothy

Squires, and is unique in that much of her story is told in her own words and recollections, owing to the copious notes I made after each conversation and rendezvous. She speaks of the men she loved and lost, in particular the songwriter Billy Reid, and the actor Roger Moore, whom she married. Alternating between sardonic wit and scathing anger, she never holds back when denouncing those who used and abused her, most especially "the establishment", and when reflecting upon her many legal battles which resulted in the High Court declaring her a vexatious litigant. Hers is a fascinating story.

I became hooked on Dorothy Squires in 1968, when she made her "comeback"—though she had never really been away—with "Your Flowers Arrived Too Late". They played the record to death on the radio, and a couple of years later, sick of being snubbed by the entertainments world, she hired the London Palladium to ultimately prove that she was still a name to be reckoned with. The show was an unprecedented success, with tickets selling out in hours and the subsequent album selling over a million copies. I first saw her on stage at the Sheffield Fiesta, shortly after my mother died. I was not yet David Bret, and my father took me to cheer me up, one of the few decent things he did in his life. I was blown away.

On 23 September 1972, with him out of my hair and now living with Jeanne, singing in the working men's clubs, and four weeks off our wedding, I went to see her again, same venue. Jeanne was not a die-hard fan, but became one when Dot sang "If You Love Me, Really Love Me", the English version of Edith Piaf's "Hymne à l'amour. When Dot had first performed this in Hollywood in the Fifties, Piaf herself had supplied the arrangement. We had it played, as

6

Jeanne walked down the aisle.

"She really *is* amazing," Jeanne enthused of the enigma in the powder-blue Douglas Darnell gown, belting out one show-stopper after another.

After the show, we decided that I wanted to meet Dot. We got backstage and a small bespectacled woman, her secretary Doris Gaard, asked us to stand outside the door at the end of the corridor. I was walking towards this when a strong hand grabbed my collar—one of the security men.

"What do you think you're playing at?" he growled.

Then all of a sudden this booming voice, "Hey, you! Get your fucking hands off him!"

This came from the tiny figure who had just emerged from the door—Dot, who had eschewed the Darnell gown for a brown skirt and cream blouse.

Over a bottle of wine, we hit it off at once. Dot arranged for us to have tickets for her show the following week, and for seventeen years we were part of her entourage. I sold albums in the foyer, Jeanne took pictures backstage for Dot's "family album". When I finished *The Piaf Legend*, she read the script before it went off to the publishers. I wrote her a song, "I Sing My Life", with the French singer, Gérard Berliner:

> *I wear my life upon my sleeve,*
> *Because I know just what it's like to take the blows,*
> *I face each storm, and I pull through*
> *Each hopeless mess of broken dreams, and I survive…*

At Dot's concerts we met dozens of celebrities and politicians along with so-called socialites she had little time for. There were nice people, such as the ailing pianist Russ

Conway, who had a different young man with him each time—two A-lister footballers who turned up with male lovers, introduced as their "personal assistants—until they had downed a few drinks, when the truth came tumbling out. There was Marion Montgomery, who along with her then performance partner, Richard Rodney Bennett, also became friends. Nicky Welsh, Dot's orchestra leader, was an absolute scream, especially after a tipple, as was Johnnie Gray, a man with a huge handlebar moustache which would have put Jimmy Edwards to shame. Then there were others who were not so nice: a soon to be well-known, over-the-top bitchy camp television presenter springs to mind, a couple of spitting-cat camp pianists, and a crooner who had seen better days but still considered himself the next best thing to Frank Sinatra. There were other celebrity Squires fanatics who, whilst raving about her, disliked one another intensely and often hissed and clawed at each other like angry snakes, backstage.

I only saw Dot lose her cool once—and I mean *really* lose it to the point of almost passing out with rage. This was in Birmingham, when she was made aware of the comment in *Cosmopolitan*—in the wake of a sustained campaign of taunts by *Private Eye*, which described Marianne Faithfull as, "Britain's most famous wreck since Dorothy Squires." Dot even broke up the editor's name to get a "fuck" between the syllables, and sued for libel. The judge, Patrick O'Connor, awarded her £8,000 in damages. Ironically, the pub that we all headed for that night after the show, the Mulberry Bush, was one of the two involved later that year in the Birmingham bombings which killed twenty-one people. It was O'Connor who presided over the appeals in 1988 of the so-called "Birmingham Six".

With Dot, life could be frantic and frustrating, but it was never dull. In her final years, she became a victim of her own insecurity and always believed that the world and its mother were out to get her. She penned her memoirs under the title, *Rain, Rain, Go Away!* These were *so* litigious that once they had been ditched by the original publisher on account of the multitude of threatened lawsuits, not least of all from Roger Moore, no publisher would touch them—whilst Dot refused to compromise and change a single word. She sent me part of the script when there was talk of me becoming her ghost-writer—a sizeable portion of this is legally paraphrased here and thus does not infringe copyright, whilst some of the chapter headings may not be repeated for legal reasons, and sometimes because their wording was *i/legal!* Dot told me much more, however, than was printed in the press at the time, well aware that I would tell her story, one day. *This* is that story....

1: Nenna

"There's something that little extra about me—like Bassey, Garland, Piaf. We've all had lousy lives. It's something you play the game for. You're a target. But outside it all, it's worth it!" Dorothy Squires, 1984.

There has been no little dissention regarding the actual date of Dorothy Squires' birth. She was definitely born on 25 March. But in which year? The record books tell us 1915, which she always denied, declaring that "a shitty journalist with an axe to grind"—mutually loathed by both of us and many of our friends—had invented this date to such an extent that it had become historical fact. In 1974, one British tabloid put her at 45, 47 and 50 in three separate features within two weeks. Dot did not help matters much that same year when by snarling at one over-inquisitive reporter, "Well, I'm not fifty. I've got a few years yet for that." Of one thing we may be certain—she was *definitely* born before 1924. In 1987, when I sent her the script I had written about Edith Piaf, she suggested that I find myself an agent and try and get it published. I did this, and it subsequently became my first book, *The Piaf Legend*, which I dedicated to her.

"I adored Piaf," Dot said. "We met a few times, and we appreciated each other's work. Who knows, if you get around to writing about me, you could dedicate *that* book to her!"

Then I made the mistake of saying that she and Piaf were around the same age, that they had cornered the market where *chanteuse-réalistes* were concerned—she in Britain, Piaf in France."

"Bollocks," she exploded. "Piaf and I were *not* the same age. I was born after her, just a little bit before one of your other singers, Patachou."

Patachou, famed in Britain not just for her sell-out cabaret appearances, but for snipping off men's neckties if they talked too much whilst she was performing, had been born 10 June 1918, whereas Piaf had entered the world on 19 December 1915. If Dot was being truthful, this would put the year of her birth between 1916 and 1918. Her passport, which she once showed me, was inscribed with the later date, and I have no reason to suspect that it had been "doctored". She did however more than occasionally "fib" about her age.

Whatever, she was born Edna May Squires—not in a trunk, as Judy Garland proclaimed in one of her most famous songs, but in a "carnival caravan" parked in Bridge Shop Field in Pontyberem, a village near Llanelli, in South Wales. In her unpublished memoirs, Dot remembers how her parents had argued because her father had wanted to call her Agnes, a name she had been saddled with until her mother suggested changing it to Edna. Dot hated the name and could never pronounce it as a child, and always insisted on being called Nenna, even when she had become Dorothy Squires.

Nenna's father, Archie, was a steelworker who worked five eight-hour shifts from Monday to Friday— and as if this was not enough on weekends he travelled around the region with a horse and cart selling fruit and vegetables. Her mother Emily (née Rickets) was "a regular housewife". There was a younger brother William, who never answered to any other name but Freddie—and an elder sister Irene, always referred to as Renee. Soon after Nenna's birth, the family left the caravan—loaned to them by Archie's father, who ran a stall at a travelling fairground—and moved in with Emily's mother, who lived at Domingo Cottage, in Dafen. Here, besides looking after her children and "fetching and carrying" for elderly relatives, Emily opened a general store—in the front room. Mrs. Rickets had also taken in another son, his wife and their young family.

"I remember Mama saying there were non-stop rows from morning until night," Dot recalled. "Who knows, maybe that's how I acquired my feisty nature!"

Archie and Emily put up with the squabbling and cramped living arrangements for several years whilst saving up to buy a place of their own. In 1928, they acquired Aston House, in New Road, Dafen, where in May 2103 a blue plaque would be unveiled in memory of its famous resident.

At the age of five, Nenna was enrolled at Dafen School. Her earliest recollection of the establishment, she said, was when she participated in a talent contest at her local church and performed her mother's favourite song, "Jealous Of You", with which she came second. This contained the line, "Maybe someday he'll turn away to somebody else that is new." Dot recalled in her memoirs that when presenting her with her prize, the vicar observed, "Let's hope that *you* never have to sing those words and cry."

Dot spoke of her father's obsession with boots—the fact that, though these were more expensive than shoes, they lasted three times as long. She remembered a school concert at the local parish hall where she played a fairy, but because she had nothing to put on but her ungainly boots, she danced in her stockinged feet. All went well until she stood on a nail and cut her foot, though she kept on dancing just the same. That night, in the bed they shared, her sister Renee rebuked her for carrying on with the performance, saying that she could have contracted blood-poisoning.

Dot recalled, "I told her, I didn't give a bugger. Well, I don't suppose I used those exact words. I told her that I didn't want to be a dancer, I wanted to be a singer. Then I raised the roof by belting out 'Jesus Wants Me For A Sunbeam', and she told me that if I didn't shut up, she would throttle me!"

From an early age, Nenna's dream was to learn to play the piano, as she explained:

> I remember my mother once asking me what I wanted for Christmas. I said I would love a piano. We were living in a biggish house by then, but she said there wasn't enough room, and that in any case we couldn't afford one. So she bought me a ukulele instead—she was a big George Formby fan, while I always found him too daft to laugh at. My idol at the time was Al Jolson.

At twelve, Nenna sat an examination so that she could attend the more prestigious Prospect Place Girls School, in Llanelli, though she was determined to stay at Dafen, where she was happy and doing well with her studies. She later said how she had done her utmost *not* to pass the examination, and that the two years she spent at Prospect Place were the most miserable of her life. At Dafen, she said, she had always been in the top ten in her class and had excelled at English, history and maths. At the new school, her confidence slumped, and in her own words she became "the dumbest of knuckleheads", good only at cooking, needlework and playing hockey. Her only consolation was singing in concerts in the local clubs and community halls—her first professional engagement, for which she was paid sixpence, saw her performing two songs at Bynea Parish Hall, accompanying herself on the ukulele.

After leaving school at fifteen, Nenna worked in a factory which manufactured tin plates, though she was still intent on having a singing career. Speaking to the Llanelli Community Heritage's Lyn John in 2011, local man Jack Davies recalled her first audience—singing on Dafen Bridge to a gang of local boys, whilst a neighbour remembered his mother telling him how Edna May Squires used to practice her song-and-ukulele routine in the outside toilet at Aston House.

Through a concert secretary friend of her father's, in 1932 Nenna began singing in working men's clubs in and around Llanelli, still accompanying herself on the ukulele. She also sang with bands appearing at Llanelli's Ritz Super Ballroom, most notably the Denza Dance Orchestra, a semi-professional outfit fronted by Len Colvin, which also played at charity events and for visiting dignitaries. She had not yet however, as some sources state, turned professional.

Dot recalled:

> My first actual job after leaving school was at Woolies [Woolworth] for all of a pound a week, and *then* at the plates factory for thirty-bob a week before applying to for a nursing course in Croydon. Then I looked around me and saw all those people stuck in dead-end jobs for the rest of their lives, and

I decided this was not for me. I told my mother, 'Bugger, I'm off to London to seek my fortune.' And when I saw how worried she looked, I added that was where the nursing course was, and that seemed to settle her.

She later told *Radio Pictorial* magazine:

Funny how elated I felt during that journey, funnier still how bewildered and lost I felt when I set foot on Paddington Station, I wanted to go straight back, only I hadn't the money to buy the ticket. In any case, having set out on this adventure, I meant to go through with it, whatever the obstacles.

This was in the summer of 1933, and as Dot was legally still a minor—eighteen, if born in 1915, younger if not—her family could have reported her as a runaway. Her mother appears to have approved of her leaving home—Dot said because she had expected her to be back within the week—but she waited until her father had left for work before setting off for London. The details of what happened next are sketchy.

"Emptying bedpans was not for me, and I soon packed it in," was all that Dot would say. "Like any other hopeful I did the rounds of the agents and lived in cheap digs, and ended up with a man—a lover who used me just as much as I used him, and who loved me as much as I did him."

In fact, Dot worked as a trainee nurse in Croydon until April 1935, always on the day shift so that her evenings were free for her to sing at local clubs. This may suggest that she *had* been born in 1915, and thus just turned eighteen, at a time when variety agents could not employ a minor without their parent's signature on the contract, whilst some were willing to waver this if the client was not eighteen, but looked it. The man Dot was referring to was Joe Kay, a 40-something variety agent whose office was in London's Charing Cross Road. Dot turned up with two pieces of sheet music: the completely forgotten "My Bleeding Heart", and Harry Akst's "Dinah", introduced by Eddie Cantor in the Broadway musical, *Kid Boots*, and subsequently popularised by Bing Crosby and Joséphine Baker. Kay was pleased with the girl and with her performance—he took her on, and they became lovers. Most importantly, Kay told her that she would never get anywhere with a name like Edna May Squires, which he said resembled that of a "washed-out silent movies star". He subsequently re-baptised her Dorothy Squires.

For several months Dot cut her teeth on the London variety scene, opening the show at minor theatres and clubs in and around London. By the end of the year, Joe Kay considered her worthy of being moved a rung up the show business ladder and acquired her an engagement at the more up-market Burlington Gardens Club. The management liked her and offered her a one-week stint, with the possibility of this being extended and of her even becoming the establishment's artiste-in-residence. Her luck changed once more during her second appearance at the venue, for the bandleader Charlie Kunz happened to be in the audience.

Pennsylvania-born Kunz (1896-1958) had started his career as a child prodigy pianist, and during World War I, whilst still in his teens and working in a munitions factory, he had founded his own dance-band. He had emigrated to England in 1921—where after a stint with Ed Krick's Dance

Band he had been engaged as pianist and later bandleader at a number of establishments, notably at Lyon's Corner House in Piccadilly, and the London Trocadero. His signature tune was "Clap Hands, Here Comes Charlie". His favourite vocalists at the time, the ones who performed with him most, were the now forgotten George Barclay and Harry Bentley—and Vera Lynn.

"I never liked her," Dot said of the Forces Sweetheart. "She had a great voice but there was never much emotion. She just stood there like a block of ice and projected no warmth. And you can bet your life that if Vera denounced a theatre of club too shitty to perform in, they gave it to me."

Many years later she told Tony Stewart of the *New Musical Express*, "I was paid off for more jobs than you could think of. I was the worst singer some bands had ever had. Jesus, it was awful."

Kunz headed for Dot's dressing room, only to learn that she and Joe Kay had left the venue immediately after her spot. The next morning he sent his secretary around to her digs with an offer she could hardly refuse: he wanted to audition her to sing with his band, currently in residence at the Casani Club, on Regent Street. Dot sang for him that afternoon, and was hired on the spot. Her first performance was scheduled for 28 February 1936, but she received a pleasant surprise when told that she would be starting work with Kunz one day earlier, replacing Vera Lynn—and that her performance was to be broadcast live on the radio by the BBC! What Vera Lynn had to say about this is not on record.

The first that Dot's parents heard about her big break was a week before the broadcast—when it was announced in the *Llanelli & County Guardian*:

> *CROONER ON THE AIR: YOUNG LLANELLYITE TO BROADCAST:* Miss Dorothy (Edna) Squires, Llanelli, who is well-known to local devotees of the Terpsichorean art, will broadcast for the first time on the National Broadcasting programme on the 27th inst. Her engagement is along with Charlie Kunz and his Dance Band on that date at the Casani Club, London, from whence the broadcast will be made. Miss Squires will enjoy the distinction of being one of the first Llanellyites to broadcast from the National Programme in this form of entertainment. She has made frequent appearances at the Ritz Super Ballroom, Llanelli, as the crooner of the Denza Players, and enjoys a large measure of popularity.

When the manager of the town's Ritz Super Ballroom read this, he contacted the Casani Club, and then Dot's digs, and invited her back to his venue. This time she would be topping the bill, and with *her* choice of orchestra—Len Colvin's Denza Dance Band, or Billy Reid's London Accordion Band, as both were on the bill. Dot plumped for the former, though it was working with the latter that would eventually propel her to world fame.

2: Billy Reid

"There are two irreconcilables in Dorothy's character: the aggressive, challenging, dominant woman who needs to be free—and the insecure, demanding woman who needs to be dependent on one man's love. These make her personal life difficult, but her performing life easy." Sally Clyde, friend.

Dot recalled the reception she received from her parents, upon her return home from London:

> I guess you could say the shit well and truly hit the fan. No one from my neck of the woods had ever taken the risks I had, and the rest of the family looked at me as if I'd grown a spare head. My father had gone down to the pub instead of listening to the broadcast, and he didn't speak to me for two days.

Their opinion changed when they turned up at the Ritz Super Ballroom—Archie with such reluctance that he had not even bothered to change out of his work clothes—and saw the place packed to the rafters, for they now realised that their daughter *had* made the right decision to go into show business.

After the show, Billy Reid approached Dot and asked her to join him on the road—the London Accordion Band were midway through a tour of England and Wales, and were scheduled to leave Llanelli the next morning. She declined, saying that she had commitments in London, and promptly returned to her lover Joe Kay, who quickly put together an eight-weeks tour—her first as a solo artiste.

Dot recalled her first lover with great affection:

> Joe was a lovely man and he always treated me kindly and had my interests at heart. But I was completely unknown in London and had no option but to work wherever they'd have me, often with a different band every night. And some of those bandleaders could be real bastards. Some of them thought that dropping your knickers after the show came part of the package and in that respect they'd picked the wrong girl. In the short time we were together, I was faithful to Joe, and I would like to think he was faithful to me.

Even so, after the tour Dot and Joe Kay parted company, and she sought out Billy Reid, who within days had assumed the role of her Svengali.

Southampton born Reid (1902-74) was perhaps the greatest bandleader of his generation, an accomplished pianist and accordionist when he met Dot in April 1936, though he was not yet into his great songwriting phase. When he boasted of how under his tutelage she would achieve great things, she was astute enough to realise that if *this* was what he thought of her, then she was worth more than the £6 a week he was willing to offer her, should she agree to sing with his London Accordion Band. She demanded £9 a week, and got it.

Dot's repertoire consisted mostly of forgettable ditties which today would be deemed corny. She had a passion for singing songs about the moon. "Moonlight On The Prairie", "Moon In The Sky" and "In The Valley Of The Moon" were three which Reid got her to drop. On the positive side, she had a fascination for songs about flowers which would stay with her for the rest of her career. With Reid she frequently opened her set with "Memory Of A Rose", livened things up a little with "When The Wild, Wild Roses Bloom", and rounded the evening off with Don Pelosi's tender anthem about lost love which would set the stall for all of her powerhouse performances of the 1970s and 1980s:

> *When the poppies bloom again, I'll remember you,*
> *There beside the River Seine, where we kissed anew,*
> *And you told me not to cry and held me tenderly,*
> *But that kiss was our goodbye,*
> *You were gone from me…*

Within weeks of taking her under his wing Reid and Dot had become lovers. She recalled in a television retrospective in 1998, shortly before her death:

> Billy Reid was a very talented man, an underestimated writer, one of the greatest we've ever had—including the Beatles. And he came up behind me one day and said, "I love you!"

By the time Dot cut her first record—"When The Poppies Bloom Again" on 6 December 1936—Reid had left his wife and set up home with her. If she was expecting special favours as the new "Mrs. Reid", however, these would not be forthcoming just yet. Despite her protests, Reid would not allow her to steal his thunder by having her name printed on the record label. The record went almost unnoticed, the "rival" version by The Radio Serenaders getting most of the airplay.

Dot was not pleased, and blamed Reid for its failure *because* he had refused to include her name on the label. Reid promised her this would easily be rectified, when they entered the studio in August 1937 to record Vincent Rose's "Moon At Sea", Ned Washington's "Sweet Heartache", and Mischa Spoliansky's "Kiss Me Goodnight" from the film, *Paradise For Two*. All were laid down in single takes, as were other numbers recorded soon afterwards, including Stanley Damerell's "Whistling Gypsy Waltz", and Don Pelosi's "Little Drummer Boy". Reid allowed Dot's name to appear on some labels, but not on all of them, and when this extended to omitting her name from some theatre bills, there was a massive bust-up between the budding star and her Svengali. Dot recalled:

> He was what you would call today a control-freak. He didn't want my name on the record labels because he didn't want it to deflect away from him. He told me what to sing, how to sing it, what to wear—even what to eat. He once followed me to the loo, to make sure I wasn't seeing someone else behind his back. So I retaliated by telling him go and fuck himself, and went back to where I'd been before we met.

This parting of the ways saw her returning to Joe Kay and taking up where they left off. Kay found work for her touring provincial theatres and munitions factories up and down the country, performing with whatever accompaniment was available—sometimes a band, more often than not with just a piano. Then, in the spring of 1945, Dot and Billy Reid were reunited. This time around the arguments would turn out to be truly spectacular—not just vociferous, but physical with punches thrown by both protagonists, often in public.

"In my book, no man ever hits a woman unless he wants a left-hook or a knee in the balls," she declared.

This time, Dot put her foot down. During the war she had amassed a sizeable following in Britain, and would no longer be content to be ignored or just referred to as "vocal refrain". Reid presented her with a song he had written, words and music, and which reflected the mood of the moment now that the war was almost over—"Coming Home"—and wanted her to record it. She agreed, but this time the label would have *her* name in capital letters, and his underneath. Reid knew that he was on to a good thing, and capitulated. A mighty but at times extremely volatile partnership had been established.

Dot and Reid hit the jackpot with the song, released three weeks after VE Day with Fred Heatherton's "Dreams Of Yesterday" on the flipside and capturing the mood of a nation when all the soldiers were returning home from the war:

> *Through the years of sadness,*
> *We've been smiling through,*
> *Waiting for the day when I'll be coming home to*
> *you.*

The song topped the Sheet Music Charts after Dot sang it on the BBC radio programme, *Variety Bandbox*. There was also a rival version by Vera Lynn.

"She sang it so *mournfully*," Dot said. "She sounded like she was falling asleep! It's no small wonder that the soldiers didn't *return* to the Front!"

"Coming Home" was very quickly followed by American bandleader Carl Ravazza's "Waiting", formerly a jazzy number which slowed down and turned into a realist song. Much better however was the flipside which received more airtime: Charles Tobias' "Just A Prayer Away", introduced by Bing Crosby the year before—and which took on a whole new meaning when, performed with a quartet of soldiers, it tugged at the heartstrings of the wives, sweethearts, families and friends of those still fighting in the Pacific.

An even more massive hit was Billy Reid's "The Gypsy", the story of a disillusioned woman who knows that her man is cheating on her, but who nevertheless visits a charlatan fortune teller who tries to convince her that he is faithful, even though they both know that he is not:

> *She looked at my hand and told me my lover was*
> *always true,*
> *But deep in my heart I knew, dear,*
> *Somebody else was kissing you…*

Even so, the woman decides she will keep going back to the gypsy because one day she hopes the man will return. The song set a precedent, in that for reasons known only to the record companies, Dot was *never* permitted to release her songs on the other side of the Atlantic until they had been covered by an American artiste:

> It was prejudice, pure and simple. Billy Reid made a fortune out of those songs because he'd written them, whereas I made nothing—and all too often suffered the indignity of the American public never knowing that they'd been created by me, but by somebody else.

Bill Kenny & The Inkspots topped the *Billboard* chart in 1946 with "The Gypsy" whilst Dinah Shore reached Number 2 with "Laughing on the Inside", another Squires song, on the flipside. To add insult to injury Shore's record company re-released the latter song as an A-side that same year, and it reached Number 3.

"I *loathed* the way they called me the American Dinah Shore," Dot scathed. "Didn't they think we had any original artists in England, without having to copy one of theirs?"

Over the next few years one Squires-Reid hit followed another. In November 1945, Dot recorded "I'll Close My Eyes" with "Let the Rest of the World Go By" on the B-side. In the original song the words and music were by Reid and it is a pastiche of loss and regret brought about by the woman who expected too much from her love affair:

> Can it be that once again, I was reaching too high?
> Love was mine, you gave me a chance,
> But my heart was not content and I lost my romance…

In the United States the song was considered "maudlin" by Buddy Kaye, perhaps best known for "Till the End of Time", based on a Chopin *polonaise*, who felt that it required new lyrics to cheer it up a little. In doing so he completely ruined it by turning it into a proclamation of fidelity—for now we have the narrator declaring that their love is expected to last for ever:

> I'll close my eyes to everyone but you,
> And when I do, I'll see you standing there…
> I'll close my eyes to everything that's gay.

Frances Langford and Andy Russell had hits with the song, but whereas the former's version is passable, Russell drones on, dirge-like. Reid objected, but as his name still appeared on the song-sheet and record label, nothing could be done. Dot for her part refused to sing the Kaye lyric in America, even when accused of changing the words herself.

"The cheek of it," she said. "Imagine what would happen if I sang a line today like 'I'll close my eyes to everything that's gay.' Those boys would throw things at me!"

But what, I asked, did she think of the later version by Joan Regan, who insisted on using the original words?

"Beautiful, like everything else she sang," Dot replied. "In my opinion, there have only been two consistently brilliant British women singers—Joan Regan and Kathy Kirby."

By natural progression, we went through a list of British

girl singers. If she gave the impression publicly of liking Alma Cogan, this was not so. She remembered appearing with her at the Prince of Wales Theatre in April 1964 in a tribute show to Michael Holliday, of whom more later:

> It's sad she died so young. But to say that she was a little on the sluttish side was an understatement. That night, backstage, she was anybody's. That's not the way a young woman should behave. She came to a couple of my parties in Bexley, it's true. But it was Roger [Moore] who invited her, never me.

Dot described Ruby Murray as "okay when she wasn't pissed out of her head." Anne Shelton she adored. Petula Clark she considered "too common", which left those who had risen to prominence during the mid-Sixties:

> Cilla Black was good with big ballads but sang down her nose. Marianne Faithful and Lulu I never classed as singers. It was obvious that Sandie Shaw would win Eurovision. It was like putting Red Rum in a one-horse Grand National. I loved Helen Shapiro and had her on the bill with me. We were told to expect a Shirley Temple prima donna. But she was a sweet thing, polite, well aware of what she wanted out of her career, so tremendously talented. I adored her. Then she disappeared just as quickly as she had arrived.

"Which leaves just Dusty Springfield," I concluded.

"The songs she was told to sing later in her career were second rate," Dot opined. "A singer has her own style which she should stick to. They wouldn't have got away with telling Bassey or me what to sing. Dusty was too soft with them."

"And Bassey?" I ventured.

"Bassey copied *me*," Dot snapped. "I never found her original, even in the slightest."

Dot's big Billy Reid songs in 1946 were "It's A Pity To Say Goodnight" and "Laughing On The Outside". "Three Beautiful Words Of Love" might have fared better had a radio programme not played the B-side by mistake. There were complaints from listeners that "My Man Didn't Come Back" was too morbid, and the record was unfairly assigned to the BBC's "banned box". Comparisons were made between it and the so-called "Budapest suicide-song", "Gloomy Sunday", banned ten years previously. Lyrically and emotionally, it is one of the finest songs that Dot performed at the time, and displays the harsh realities of war—that not every soldier's story ended happily as the one in "Coming Home":

> *Romance was ours, we were so in love…*
> *The world went crazy,*
> *And the shadows came to take away the sun above…*
> *My man didn't come back, I miss him night and day,*
> *To give us peace and freedom, somebody else had to pay…but who am I to complain?*
> *As long as what he fought for can never happen again.*

Next off the Reid-Squires assembly line was "A Tree In The Meadow" which came about as a result of Dot and Reid having a row whilst driving through the countryside.

"Billy was a genius when it came to writing songs," Dot said. "He was also a very unpredictable man and you never knew when he was going to snap. Yes, he used to hit me but he soon stopped when I began hitting him back."

During their bust-up, matters became so inflamed that Reid lost control of the wheel and ploughed the car through a fence into a field, stopping inches off crashing into a tree.

"We got out to check the damage," Dot added. "Then Billy forgot all about that when he saw the big heart carved into the tree-trunk, with the lover's initials. It didn't stop us rowing all the way home, though."

Dot recorded the song in January 1948. It was a big hit in Britain and there was talk of an American tour, which was shelved when Dot learned that Margaret Whiting had taken her version of the song to the top of the *Billboard* charts. "My Mother's Day", recorded in October 1948, was one of only two records by British female singers that Elvis Presley kept on his jukebox. The other was Cilla Black's "You're My World". Before fame prohibited him from going far without the protection of the so-called "Memphis Mafia", he and his mother Gladys often went to see Dot's shows in Hollywood. But, was the song really about Dot's own mother, or Reid's?

"No," was Dot's response. "Many songs in those days were overly sentimental—kitschy. 'China Girl Meets China Girl' was another. Coming so soon after the war, sentiments were running high. Sons were praising the mothers they thought they'd never see again. 'Mother's Day' managed to stay in the public conscience, while most of the others were quickly forgotten."

Dot and Billy Reid lived openly, as couple, from the end of the war until 1951, attracting a great deal of criticism from moralists. She made it clear from the start of their relationship, however, that he would never own her and that she had no intention of performing exclusively with him—that every now and then she should be free to work as a solo artiste. She also persistently told reporters that she was not British, but Welsh, and made a point of returning to her homeland as often as she could. She did a great deal of charity work in her homeland to raise funds for the Nuffield Works Hospital, and regularly topped the bill at the Llanelli Odeon—the cinema she said had started it all off when she had seen Al Jolson in *The Jazz Singer*. She topped the bill at the London Palladium and became a regular on the BBC radio show, *Variety Bandbox.*

Compered by Philip Slessor (until Derek Roy replaced him), *Variety Bandbox* was first broadcast by the Light Programme in 1941 and became a British institution—*the* programme which everyone tuned into on Sunday evenings, with its eclectic mixture of comedy, music and song and which launched a host of performers who became household names. Peter Sellers, Arthur English, Tony Hancock, Miriam Karlin and Frankie Howerd started here—or were given boosts to careers which otherwise might not have happened. Eric Sykes worked as a scriptwriter. The most popular with listeners however were the orchestras of Ted Heath, Geraldo, Ambrose and Billy Reid with their resident vocalists. Over the next few years, Dot and Reid also featured regularly on all the other big radio shows: *Variety Fanfare*, *Henry Hall's Guest Night*, *All Star Bill*, *Melody Lane*, and *Band Parade.*

In September 1949, accompanied by Reid and his orchestra, Dot performed twenty of his songs at the Regal Cinema in Dafen, where it was standing-room only. Such was her reception that she told Reid she was seriously thinking of coming back here to live. This dream was partially realised in February 1950 when they purchased the Astoria Theatre, on Llanelli's New Dock Road. Built in 1913, this seated around 1,000 people and once Dot had paid for it to be refurbished, the acoustics were such that she was able to make herself heard at the back of the hall without having to use the sound system. The exercise was short-lived, when Dot was revealed to be Britain's highest-paid singer. Reid drilled it into her that it would be impossible to run a successful career so far from London, and though they retained the property for now, she and Reid bought a 16-room house on St Mary's Mount, Bexley, Kent. Until now, they had lived at his house on Chaucer Road, in Brixton's Herne Hill district.

Dot's and Reid's stormy relationship was thrown a lifeline, albeit briefly, when during the summer of 1950 they

29

were asked to do a series of shows in Turkey. "A Tree In The Meadow" and "Mother's Day" had proved popular here, but when radio listeners were asked to name their favourite Dorothy Squires song topping the poll was "I'm In The Mood For Love" which Parlophone had put out in 1947 on the flipside of Reid's "I'm Gonna Hold You In My Arms". They re-recorded this and it was released in Turkey by Odeon, with "Wilhemina" on the flipside—performed not by Dot, but by Larry Macari and The Dutch Serenaders, with whom they shared top-billing during the tour which took in clubs, theatres and radio stations in Istanbul and Ankara.

"Wilhemina" had been performed by Betty Grable in the film, *Wabash Avenue*, which was released in Turkey shortly before Dot arrived there. When it was suggested that Grable had lyp-synched to Dot's voice in the film—she had not—she was asked to perform it time and time again, not with Reid but with Macari, which did little to help ease the tension.

I asked her if she had ever wanted to go back to Turkey and her sharp response was, "No way. *What* a bloody hole *that* was!"

Upon the couple's return to England there were more rows than ever before, until they finally threw in the towel after a nasty fight in the bar in the Astoria's Theatre bar, when Reid hit Dot once too often and she laid into him. Her father came off worst when he tried to separate them and was hit by a stray punch. This acrimony persisted for several years, resulting in a heated exchange at London's High Court in March 1958 over who should own what, and when both parties were warned that they would be held in contempt of court unless they calmed down. An estate agent commissioned by the court had valued the Bexley house at £8,600. Reid claimed that he and Dot owned equal shares and applied for an injunction to prevent her from selling it without his consent. Dot provided papers proving that *she* had bought the house. The judge decreed that she should keep it, whilst Reid would retain the Astoria

Theatre. Ten years later, this was converted into a bingo hall like many cinemas up and down the country. What is interesting is that Dot was asked her age, and responded under oath that she was two weeks off her thirtieth birthday, which ties in with my theory that she was born in 1918, and not three years earlier.

Reid stalked Dot for some time, despite being warned by the police to keep away from her. There were reports of him parking his car out of sight and watching the guests arriving at her parties, trying to work out if any of the men visiting St Mary's Mount might have been sleeping with her. On one occasion he turned up in the middle of the night and, seeing a light on in her bedroom, managed to find a ladder in one of the outbuildings and climbed up to see if she had company.

Dot later told Anne de Courcy, "Though I never gave him cause to be jealous, he had me followed. Finally, I just couldn't go on with it."

To the *NME*'s Tony Stewart she opened up a little more:

> I don't have very fond memories of that time because it was a very turbulent period of my life. I was emotionally involved with that man, and he had insane jealousies. I literally couldn't go anywhere. And when you're distrusted in that way it just drives you up the bloody wall. So I just got in my car one day and drove away.

Billy Reid continued writing songs for Dot for a few more years, until his career slumped—on account of the pop boom of the 1960s when his music was deemed to be old-fashioned. The man who had made millions at the height of his success died, bankrupt and penniless, in December 1974 aged seventy-two, largely forgotten but for the songs he had written for his ever-grateful protégée, who never stopped praising him and performing his work in her shows.

Dot's first publicity photograph, c.1937

3: Roger

"I don't think you can develop a charisma. Either you have it or you don't have it, and she had it." Roger Moore.

Dot's father, her sister Renée and Renée's husband Dai moved in to look after St Mary's Mount whilst she was on the road, and each time she returned home there were lavish parties. It was at one of these, in 1952, that she met an aspiring young actor and model named Roger Moore. For Dot, and for those who knew her and were compelled to live through the ensuing catalogue of triumphs, traumas and tribulations, life would never be the same again.

Roger Moore was born on 14 October 1927 in London's Stockwell district, the only child of George, a policeman, and Lillian (Pope). After spending part of the war as an evacuee in Cornwall, he had returned to London and at sixteen the acting bug had bitten when he had been sponsored to serve two terms at RADA by the film director, Brian Desmond Hurst. Belfast-born Hurst (1895-1986) was a promiscuous homosexual with a penchant for much younger men, and over the years there has been speculation over whether this might have been the reason for his taking Moore under his wing. In his memoirs, Moore recalls how Hurst made a point of telling his theatrical friends, most of whom were gay, that his protégé was "not that way inclined". He also remembers the occasion when he visited Hurst's Belgravia home.

"I don't know if this was a test to see if I had any gay tendencies," he writes. "I found myself seated on one of those Knole settees between Godfrey Winn, a well-known writer, and playwright Terence Rattigan."

Moore remembers Winn suggestively telling him that when in his early twenties, *he* had been the most beautiful man in London—to which Moore had replied, effecting a deep voice, "I am not queer, you know!" He concludes that during the obvious embarrassing silence that had followed, Winn had scratched his head and Rattigan had started to say something, whilst Hurst had worn a great grin on his face.

"I don't mean to sound homophobic," Moore concluded. "I'm not. But back then I was—as they say—a red-blooded male eager to prove my manhood. I'd rather hoped to receive such adulation from members of the *opposite* sex!"

Dot was no longer with us when Moore published his book, but back in 1972 she did express an opinion:

> I think Roger may have flirted with him, innocently and in appreciation for all that Hurst did for him—the gifts he lavished on him. Did they take things to the next level? I never asked him! But who knows what a young man might do to get along in the world? I'm certain that it was all platonic, but if it wasn't he wouldn't have been the first, and he certainly won't be the last.

Hurst confirmed this (Christopher Robbins: *The Empress of Ireland*), saying, "Everyone thinks that Roger and I were lovers, but Roger Moore is not like that."

Moore always said that he had left RADA to find work as an actor, which on the face of it sounds odd because this was why he had enrolled in the first place. It may well have been that his admiration for Hurst had been mistaken for something else by the director, and that Moore realised this and felt the need to distance himself from him. Perhaps we shall never know. In 1945/6, Moore appeared as an extra in four films, the best-known being *Caesar and Cleopatra* with Vivien Leigh and Stewart Granger. Towards the end of 1945, he was called up for national service and in September 1946 was commissioned into the Royal Army Service Corps, as second lieutenant. Promoted to captain, he transferred to Hamburg, in Germany, where he looked after artistes entertaining the armed forces. In the December of this year, Moore married RADA student and ice skater Doorn Van Steyn (Lucy Woodward, 1922-2010), five years his senior. The couple initially lived with her family in Streatham, and allegedly blamed the collapse of their marriage on money problems and Van Steyn's lack of confidence in him ever making the grade as an actor. Moore also confessed to having been the victim of domestic violence. He met Dot courtesy of mutual friends, Betty and Lee Newman, who at some time had lived in the same house as Doorn.

In his memoirs he recalls, "The people I met there were fascinating—entirely different from my friends in rep and West End theatre. The old saying 'there's no business like show business' couldn't be truer when it came to Dot. I was now mingling with top musicians, comics and agents in the most glorious of surroundings."

Dot's account of their meeting, in her memoirs, is more impassioned. At the beginning of the section she promises the reader that her "happy pen" will tell of their first rendezvous, whilst her "sad pen" must regrettably lament their parting. Her story coincides with Moore's, save that she adds how he was initially reticent to be in such opulent surroundings. She asked him if he wanted a drink, she goes on—and he declined saying he had an ulcer, bringing the response that from her that ulcers were currently the rage. She recalls him asking her to dance—which saw her feigning indifference and telling her secretary, when it seemed likely Moore would be staying the night, that he could sleep in the stables for all she cared! She told me:

> I was playing hard to get, and I guess I was being pretty rude about it. He wasn't just handsome, he was *beautiful*. I asked myself, what the *hell* does he see in me? Then I came to one conclusion—that he

35

could only have been a gigolo. Then when all the guests had left, we were having tea in the lounge. He took one sip from his cup, then put it down. A moment later he'd gathered me up in his arms and was carrying me upstairs…"

News of Moore's relationship with Dot was quickly conveyed to his wife, and Doorn filed for divorce, citing Dot as "the other woman". Moore had also stayed in touch with Brian Desmond Hurst, which suggests that they had not fallen out as some have suggested. Since appearing in the role of "Stage Door Johnny" in the 1949 comedy musical *Trottie True*, with Jean Kent, there had been other parts for the BBC, though nothing of great significance.

"Roger appeared to be getting nowhere with his acting career and modelling work, so I decided to take him to the States see if things would be better for him over there," Dot recalled.

The modelling work amounted to little more than posing in sweaters on the covers of knitting patterns, earning Moore the nickname "The Big Knit", and appearing in toothpaste adverts. But why, so soon after meeting him and announcing their engagement, did Britain's most popular female singer turn her back on her country and head for America? Was it *really* only with the intention of launching his career, whilst risking her own.

"Of course not," she revealed. "Every song that Billy Reid wrote for me, somebody over there had nicked. "So I decided to go over there and nick a few of theirs!"

This was true. American singers *were* stealing her songs, courtesy of Reid who was making deals behind her back with record companies, and earning a fortune whilst pretending to denounce these copy-cats. Listeners began speculating about the singer who had first introduced them when disc-jockeys began playing the imported originals on the radio. However, as Americans were more moral than their British counterparts—and it had not gone unnoticed that Roger Moore *was* still married—this meant that he and Dot would have to keep their relationship under wraps.

"His wife had no faith in his acting abilities," Dot said. "I knew that he had something to offer. And what better way of getting him noticed than by taking him to America?"

There is little doubting that, even so soon in their relationship, Dot was paranoid about losing him.

"Maybe he hadn't been around that much, but wherever he went he was surrounded by pretty women," she said. "I guess it was always a question of time. I knew that, but didn't want to admit it to myself, I suppose."

Moore was what the Americans called "a pretty boy", by no means a criticism of his sexuality or any suggestion that he was anything but heterosexual. Dot was aware that, as had happened with Billy Reid, there was every chance of their age difference causing problems along the way. Reid however had not been possessed of matinee idol looks, and in this respect New York, and eventually Hollywood, was the very *last* place she needed to be taking him. Her closest friends, Diana Dors and comedienne Hylda Baker, begged her not to leave Britain. Dot, setting a precedent, refused to listen, though they at least talked her out of putting up her house for sale.

Moore's wife granted him a divorce, and he and Dot were married in New Jersey on 6 July 1953, both said by a drunken Justice of the Peace. Joe Latona—of the trio Warren, Latona & Sparks who had appeared with Dot during her last British tour—was best man. Oddly there were no photographs and she later confessed that she had been in a grumpy mood throughout the ceremony because her shoes, bought at the last minute from the bargain basement at Gimball's department store, had been one size too small and crippling her. According to Moore, the Justice of the Peace opted for the "casual approach", pronouncing, "Do you, Dot, take Rog? And Joe, will you sign here?"

In retrospect, one might almost say that the marriage was doomed from the start. Yet despite their stormy relationship, with major faults on both sides, Moore has always spoken kindly about her, and the nearest Dot ever got to criticising him was during one of our "car chats" when she recalled:

> Roger would have been nothing without me. And I would have never survived back then without him. He used me as a bank, but I *wanted* him to use me as a bank. I spent everything I'd earned over the last seven years trying to get him launched, and when he waltzed me down the aisle I only had a few dollars left to my name...

In Hollywood, where glamour frequently came before acting talent—and Dot had glamour by the ton—she was approached by several agents eager to get her into films. She turned them down because, she said, her only interest was in being a wife. In her memoirs, she confesses that for her new husband she had been ready to give up *everything,* how she had not even cared if she stepped on to another stage or not because from now on, *Roger* would be the star in the family. She also writes how there is no applause for being a wife, that the time soon came for her to choose between her public and personal life—that there was no question of her being devoted to both. One gets the impression that she was clinging to Moore not just because she was infatuated with him, but because even so soon in their marriage she was terrified what she deemed to inevitable—losing him to someone else.

The roar of this applause was too strong for her to ignore—and the fact that *she* was the breadwinner. There was no honeymoon. The very day after their wedding, Dot flew to London to begin a three months sell-out tour of the provinces. Britain of course was where she was a household name and in her element *because* she was a household name, whereas comparatively few Americans had heard of her. Indeed, in her rare early television appearances Stateside she was accused of eschewing original material for songs already made famous by American entertainers. Nothing could have been further from the truth. These *were* her songs, gazumped and hailed by the cover artists as their own. Now, with an ocean between them, all that kept her going, she said, was the endless succession of love-letters from her husband.

Moore had met Jeffrey Hunter whilst working out at a London gym. The American actor was preparing for *Sailor of the King* which required him to be shirtless much of the time and Moore was understudying one of the leads in the West End play, *The Little Hut*, a role which demanded he wear a loincloth. The pair had become friends and it was Hunter and his wife Barbara Rush who took Dot and Moore in when they were reunited after Dot's tour, and they flew to Hollywood to set about looking for an apartment in the Westwood area. Dot, picking up the tabs, settled on a place in Gayley Avenue, a neighbourhood much favoured by UCLA students.

Though but one decidedly handsome young acting hopeful amongst many, Moore had little difficulty finding work in Hollywood, with or without Dot's help. In the spring of 1953 he appeared in two episodes of NBC's Hallmark Hall of Fame: *Julius Caesar* and *Black Chiffon*, and these were followed by appearances in *Robert Montgomery Presents*: *The Wind Cannot Read* and *World by the Tail*. It was his portrayal of Joshua Wedgewood in the television movie, *The Clay of Kings*, that brought him to the attention of MGM, who contracted him for a sizeable part in *The Last Time I Saw Paris*, based on F Scott Fitzgerald's *Babylon Revisited*. In this, as lothario tennis player Paul Lane he gets to flirt with Elizabeth Taylor—and to fight with her on-screen love interest, Van Johnson. The film was directed by Richard Brooks. But if Moore and Dot were hoping to be flown to Paris for the locations, they were to be disappointed because all of his scenes were shot on an MGM backlot.

By now, Dot had added an important song to her repertoire, her most portentous so far, though not intentionally so. Cynics assumed that she had already glimpsed into the future and was having second thoughts about her marriage. She explained:

> I *had* reservations. There'd been the big final bust up with Billy Reid, part of which had to do with him being much older than me. And now there was Roger, who was much younger than *me*, and already with one failed marriage behind him. Yet despite the animosity there had once been between us, Billy was still writing songs for me. I guess with this one he saw what was coming.

The song was Reid's "I'm Walking Behind You", which tells

the story of the woman who attends the wedding of the man she has lost—and whilst walking behind him subconsciously tells him that if things do not work out with his wife, then she will take him back!

In fact, Reid had *not* written the song for Dot, but for Jimmy Young, who recorded it in February 1953. It had then been picked up by Frank Sinatra, who had recorded a cover version one week before Eddie Fisher, who took the record to Number One on both sides of the Atlantic. Dot's recording, with Reid and his orchestra, was laid down in a single take in April 1953 and backed with his "Is There Any Room In Your Heart?", and was her first for Polygon, one of Britain's first independent labels. For a while she had been unhappy with Columbia's handling of her releases, blaming them for "conspiring" with Billy Reid and handing her songs to American artistes. As such she had been approached by Leslie Clark—Petula's father, who had founded Polygon in 1949 to handle his daughter's recording career.

Dot's reasons for wanting to leave Columbia were not entirely valid, for it was *Reid* who had given her songs to her American counterparts. As for "I'm Walking Behind You", she did not mind Sinatra covering the song, but she was upset over Eddie Fisher's unprecedented success with the record.

"I met him in America," she said. "I found him sleazy—a real piece of shit. Okay, so Billy Reid didn't write the song especially for me. But if I'd still been with him, it *would* have been *exclusively* mine. And revenge was so very sweet!"

Dot's "revenge", having learned that Fisher had gazumped "her" song, was to inform Leslie Clark that she did not want Reid's name on the record label. He obliged and this reads, "With Orchestral Accompaniment".

Another song, even more portentous because in *this* one the woman does not mind her lover actually *dying,* as long as she could die too, was the English version of Edith

Piaf's "Hymne à l'amour". This was the intensely powerful chanson-réaliste which she had written in memory of her lover, the boxer Marcel Cerdan, killed in a plane crash in October 1949. Piaf had recorded the song in May 1950, and her new lover, the American tough-guy actor Eddie Constantine, had provided her with an English adaptation, "Hymn to Love".

Dot and Piaf, who met several times in Hollywood, had a tremendous admiration for each other. Piaf had imported Dot's recordings from England, and had considered asking her friend, singer-composer Charles Aznavour, to adapt 'I'll Close My Eyes' into French, inasmuch as he had recently adapted Frankie Laine's "Jezebel". Dot recalled:

> I was appearing in cabaret. I had no idea she was in the theatre that evening and I sang "Hymne à l'amour" in English. When she walked into my dressing-room afterwards I was terrified, even more so when she told me she didn't care for my arrangement. Then before I could offer my excuses she said, 'But you've got a lovely voice. Don't worry, I'll write an arrangement for you myself!' That's exactly what she did. Nothing big-bandish, just a sincere, heartfelt arrangement which I recorded the following year. After her death, I did my own arrangement of "If You Love Me, Really Love Me" and included it in the autograph sequence in my concerts. She really did hold the audience in the palm of her tiny hand. I also learned a lot from her about lighting, and years later when I was hiring the halls myself, and effectively my own boss, I put all she had taught to me to good use. I think that along with Judy Garland, she's the best woman singer this world's ever known!

Dot had recorded two other songs during her first session for Polygon, besides "I'm Walking Behind You" and its B-side. These were "Sorrento And You", and the curiously-titled "From Your Lips To The Ears Of God", released as a single in September 1953 and which seems to have vanished without trace. The Piaf song, however, was important enough for Dot to wish to fly to London—alone— to record it and several other songs for future release. Because she was missing Roger Moore so much, her visit to her homeland was brief and in three studio sessions besides the Piaf song she recorded five more, of which "It's The Talk Of The Town" may well be the only one remembered by fans today.

In Hollywood, Dot enjoyed no small amount of success on the cabaret circuit, particularly at the Moulin Rouge. Formerly the Earl Carroll Theater, this had been taken over by Frank Sennes in 1953, and like the Versailles—Piaf's first port of call when visiting America—soon developed into a celebrity watering hole because most fans could not afford the steep prices. Dot found herself rubbing shoulders with Doris Day, Gary Cooper, Liberace, Rock Hudson, Peggy Lee, Humphrey Bogart and Lauren Bacall to name but a few…and Elvis Presley—who five years later had her recording of "Mother's Day" installed in his jukebox at Graceland, in memory of his mother, Gladys. Dot and Elvis met several times at the Moulin Rouge though sadly there are no pictures of them together.

Within days of being reunited with Moore after her trip to London, Dot became convinced that he had been cheating on her during her absence. In her memoirs, by which time their marriage had long been over, she confirms that he wrote to her once, often twice a day. She admits to having kept all of his letters, and to have read them time and time again—weeping over what had been. Whilst she had been away, the neighbours in their apartment block had prayed that she would never return, she writes, for they had endlessly complained about the noise—the television always blaring out full-blast, the parties that sometimes raged on until dawn, but above all the noise the couple made whilst having sex.

"One couple accosted me in the lift," she told me. "You only had to look at them to know that they had no idea what sex was. So I said to them, 'Instead of complaining about us fucking, why don't you go and fuck yourselves?' They never complained again after that."

Early in 1954, Dot received a visit from Maxene and LaVerne Andrews, whose proposal she said "knocked her sideways":

> The Andrews Sisters and I shared a song, which they recorded but I never did. They'd had a bust-up with their sister, Patty, and wanted me to join them and go on tour. I was flattered. They were an amazing act, but our styles were so different and it wouldn't have worked. Not wishing to hurt their feelings, I told them that I would think about it.

The song was Henri Betti's "Maitre Pierre", written for Les Compagnons de la Chanson (who recorded "Les trois cloches" with Edith Piaf) and adapted into English by Mitch Parish as "The Windmill Song". Patty Andrews had wed the trio's pianist Walter Weschler in 1952 and he had taken over as their manager. When LaVerne and Maxene read in the press that Weschler was asking promoters behind their backs for more money for Patty than *they* were being paid, this caused a rift, and lawsuits began flying back and forth.

44

When Dot rejected their offer, LaVerne and Maxine continued as a duo until the end of 1954 when Maxine was hospitalised after overdosing on sleeping pills. The sisters made up and reformed in 1956, only to find their kind of harmonising overshadowed by rock-and-roll and pop.

Another celebrity fan who attended Dot's shows was the controversial stand-up comedian, Lenny Bruce (1925-66), though the admiration was far from mutual. Dot had a ribald sense of humour and could "eff and peff" with the best of them. In his book, Roger Moore recalls an incident when they were in the audience at one of his shows and Bruce made a derogatory remark about the London Palladium: "Suddenly, to my horror, Dorothy, who had by now consumed three large gin-and-tonics, screamed, 'You'd like the fucking chance to play there...you cunt!"

Though I never heard Dot use the "C" word, I can picture the scenario only too well!

In July 1955, Leslie Clark contacted Dot to announce that Polygon was about to be sold to Nixa Records, an offshoot of Pye Records. She flew to London, and her last studio session with the label produced four songs accompanied by the Radio Revellers—of these, "With All My Heart" would remain in her repertoire for another thirty years:

> With all my heart I love you,
> With all my heart, I care,
> In all the world there's no one,
> No one with you can compare...

In Britain, Dot embarked on a provincial tour and whilst deliberating over her Pye-Nixa contract she was offered deals by Decca for British recordings, and London Records for American releases. It was at around this time that she met and formed a songwriting partnership with Eddie Dunstall, a Squires stalwart who would stay with her until the end. Together they composed "Eventide" and "Set Me Free", both recorded for Decca, whilst Dot recorded Dunstall's "Coquette" and "Precious Love" for London… before deciding that she did not really want to stay with either company and signed the contract with Pye-Nixa, her reason for returning to England in the first place.

Dot with Joe Kay, c.1944

Dot and Billy Reid, c.1950, judging a beauty contest.

In Hollywood, 1953

March 1958, at the High Court, for the
property dispute hearing with Billy Reid.

At St Mary's Mount with Roger Moore, c.1959.

1960: With Roger at the *Spartacus* premiere.

Dot said that in this picture, snapped in New York
in 1960, she is only pretending to be happy

4: The Road Gets Rougher

"Life for her is never dull or uneventful. Sometimes mad. Frequently traumatic. It is tears or triumphs. Her energy and metabolism is such that God help us all if ever she were to swallow a pep pill." James Green, *London Evening News*.

By the autumn of 1955 cracks had already begun forming in the Squires-Moore marriage—Dot said because they were spending too much time apart now that he was acquiring a name for himself in Hollywood, whilst she had resumed her British career as if she had never been away. In common with her idol, Edith Piaf, Dot wore her heart on her sleeve and was always willing to share the ups and downs of her private life and her innermost thoughts with her devoted public. Therefore her first recording for Pye-Nixa, Don Pelosi's "When You Lose The One You Love", was of great significance:

> *Friends may smile at you and say that time can heal your pain,*
> *You'll fall in love again,*
> *But in your heart you know it can never be so…*

"Yes, there were problems," Dot recalled. "I guess I should have known when I married such a beautiful man that I would have trouble holding on to him. We also both wanted children, which never happened."

Dot reiterated this in her last interview for BBC Wales:

I wanted a baby. I'd had by fallopian tubes blown in

51

England but it wasn't a success, so I had them done again in Beverly Hills. I was carrying for two or three months. I came back from a piano lesson one day and Roger picked me up. He always had a habit of driving right up to the car in front, and I had a whiplash. When I got home I lost it.

Roger Moore observed in the same television retrospective of her life, *Rain, Rain Go Away: The Dorothy Squires Story*, "Dorothy would have been a wonderful mum. She was very warm, very outgoing, larger than life."

Around this time, Dot told the *Daily Mail*'s Anne de Courcy, "This man prescribed Roger tablets which he used to call 'baby pills'. He had to take two a day, I remember. But it didn't do any good."

Meanwhile, in December 1955 her brother Freddie died of kidney disease, aged just thirty-five, leaving behind a widow, Joyce, and small daughter, Emily Jane.

"We never got along," Dot recalled of her sister-in-law. "She was a hoofer and a pantomime dame, and not a very good one. I never forgave her for carrying on working the day after Freddie died. Emily was okay, but over the years our relationship has had more ups than downs. I think it's best we leave it there for now."

Early in 1956 the French singer Francis Lemarque attended one of Dot's concerts in London and a few days later—having heard of her troubles with the men in her life—presented her with "Someone To Love", the English adaptation of his recent hit, "Seul un homme peut faire ça". This declares that while there are many things that only men can do—such as building houses—there are many more things that only *women* can do, such as transforming the house into a home as long as there is a man around for her to love. Lemarque's song, one of fourteen sides she cut over the coming year for Pye-Nixa, could have seen her hitting the big time on the Continent. She was contacted by Bruno Coquatrix, the manager of the Paris Olympia who offered her a season at arguably one of the most prestigious music-halls in Europe, opening the show for either Edith Piaf or Patachou. In preparation for this, French Vogue released the song along with three others on an EP, and it was a minor hit. Not that this made any difference to Dot, who rejected Coquatrix's offer.

"I turned him down," she said. "I told him, 'I'm topping the bill all over England. Why would I want to open the show for somebody else, singing just three songs?'"

French impresarios have very long memories, and Dot was one of only two British female singers to find herself blacklisted by the "establishment" there—the other was Cilla Black, whose manager Brian Epstein boasted in November 1963 that once Cilla "hit France" she would take over where Piaf had left off and become an even bigger star than she had been—not a wise statement, just weeks after Piaf's death, when the country was still in mourning.

Unfazed, Dot made what would be her only major feature film. In 1948, there had been a guest appearance alongside Billy Reid in *Wit and Wisdom*, a television vehicle featuring Norman Wisdom of which almost nothing is known. Now, she was approached by director Maurice Elvey to play the second female lead in *Stars in Your Eyes*. Elvey, claimed to have been the most prolific director in British cinema history with almost two-hundred productions to his name, is perhaps best-known for being at the helm of Gracie Fields' first film, *Sally in Our Alley* (1931).

Dot's love interest in the storyline was New York-born actor Bonar Colleano. The female lead was Pat Kirkwood whose husband, Hubert Gregg, wrote the script. It was not a great vehicle by any means, and so far as is known has never been released on video and DVD, or even shown on British television. One might even venture to say that it is important only because Dorothy Squires is in it.

In 2000, I interviewed Pat Kirkwood for my biography of George Formby—in 1939, aged eighteen, she had been his leading lady in *Come On George!*—and during our conversation, Dot's name had come up:

> *Stars In Your Eyes* was a poor film I must admit, but it was one I was particularly proud of because it gave me the opportunity to work alongside Bonar Colleano and Dorothy Squires. Dot was a darling. She and I got on well, on the set and socially. But oh, she *never* stopped talking about Roger Moore. She was *obsessed* with talking about him to the point that it sometimes became tiresome listening to her. It was obvious they were having problems. Their marriage was doomed from the start. I'm sure of that. Maybe had there been children, there may have been a little something left to salvage, though even then I'm sure that not far into the future Dot would have found herself replaced by a younger, less-possessive woman...

The storyline of the film is basic. As more and more stage stars are falling by the wayside with the advent of television, a group of entertainers club together and buy a run-down theatre to showcase their various talents. As was usual with this type of film, a bunch of crooks try to thwart their plans, but all ends well in the end. Also in the production were the comics Jimmy Clitheroe and Nat Jackley, radio presenter Jack Jackson, and Joan Sims in an early role. Dot plays Ann Hart, the ex-wife of an alcoholic songwriter, played by Colleano. The two became close during shooting, and she was devastated two years later when Colleano was killed in a car crash near Birkenhead, aged just thirty-four.

At the time of his death, Colleano was deeply in debt, and in December 1958 it was Dot who suggested organising a celebrity football match to raise funds to help support his widow, the actress Susan Shaw, and their three-year-old son. This took place at Hayes Stadium, in Middlesex. Alma Cogan kicked off the match, where the "footballers" included actors James Mason, Alfie Bass, Sid James and Stanley Baker.

By this stage in her career, Dot was writing some of her own songs. Eventually, there would be over a hundred. Her first published composition was "Maid of the Valley", in 1953, penned under her own name.

"Nobody took any notice of that one, so I decided that after that I would use a pseudonym," she said.

There would be several of these. As "Emily Jane"—her mother's names—she wrote "Come Home to My Arms", and presented it to the Beverley Sisters. Several songs—including the first version of "With All My Heart" which she performs in *Stars in Your Eyes*—were published under the pseudonym "David Lee". She also published several songs under her married name, purposely misspelling it as "More".

Whilst making the film, Dot discovered that she was two

months pregnant, and writes in her memoirs how thrilled her husband was when she called him in Hollywood with the news. She recalls that he was giddy with excitement over becoming a father. Yet just days after shooting wrapped, she collapsed at home with agonising pains, and was rushed to hospital where she suffered another miscarriage. Her doctor advised her against getting pregnant again, warning her that it was extremely unlikely that she would ever carry full-term.

In the spring of 1957, Dot and Roger Moore flew back to England, where he had been contracted to play the lead in the 39-part television swashbuckling adventure series, *Ivanhoe*, for Columbia Pictures. Geared towards a younger audience, this following in the stamp of the top-rating *Adventures of Robin Hood* and *The Adventures of Sir Lancelot*, but with a bigger budget, and was a co-production with the studio's subsidiary company, Screen Gems, with the tetchy producer Sydney Box at the helm. Some of the interiors were shot in California, but the majority of the series was filmed at Elstree and on location in Buckinghamshire. Dot composed the theme-song, "Ivanhoe Of England", to be played over the opening and closing credits, whilst Moore supplied the lyrics. Director Arthur Crabtree loved the song and wanted to use it, but he was overruled by Box, who commissioned Louis Levy to supply the one which was performed by a male choir. Dot recorded "Ivanhoe Of England", but to date is has never been released commercially.

Just weeks into shooting the series, Moore fell ill with a suspected duodenal ulcer and production was held up whilst he recuperated. Dot decided that two weeks in the sun would be the best cure so they flew to Torremolinos, in

Spain, where she rented a villa from two fans. The place was no more than a hamlet back then, a far cry from the sprawling tourist attraction of today, but Dot fell in love with it and would return time and time again. Whilst here, under the pen name "Juanita Claros", she wrote "Torremolinos" one of her less memorable songs, a syrupy ditty which quickly dated.

In August 1957, Dot began rehearsals for what would have been her most extensive tour to date: shows in Southampton, Blackpool, Morecambe and Walthamstow, followed by week-long stints in Coventry, Liverpool, Birmingham, Stockton, Glasgow and Manchester, and finishing off with two weeks at the London Hippodrome. No sooner had she arrived than she became involved in the first of many incidents which saw her not holding back when expressing her opinion, and almost always when *she* was in the right. This resulted a vociferous spat with the promoter Harold Davison and a young American singer whom she accused of stealing her limelight.

"The Americans had done me over by nicking my songs," she recalled. "I wasn't going to be done over again by some fucking upstart I'd never heard of!"

Davison was one of Britain's most eminent impresarios who had introduced many of the big American stars to British audiences. The "upstart" was Charlie Gracie, a 21-year-old Philadelphia-born contemporary of Eddie Cochrane who since being engaged for the summer tour with Dot had scored two UK chart successes, most recently with "Fabulous" which had peaked at Number 8. When Davison had booked Dot for the tour, scheduled to open in Southampton on 4 August *she* was topping the bill.

Now, on account of Gracie's recordings being played to death on the radio, Davison affected an unwise swapping around of the bill and gave Gracie equal top-billing. Dot was fine with this, until just days before the 7 August premiere at the London Hippodrome, when Davison moved Gracie to the *top* of the bill—and demoted Dot to his support act. Quite understandably, she was furious.

She recalled, "I said to Harold Davison, 'Who the fuck is this man? I've never even heard of him.' And when he refused to listen, I did what had to be done and pulled out of the tour."

From their respective corners, Dot and Gracie battled it out in the press. She told the *Daily Sketch*:

> It's disgraceful that a British star should be treated this way. I've been in America for four years, starred in Los Angeles, and never heard of this Mr. Gracie. And I'm not being catty. I accepted this shared top billing because that is the only way a British star can get into the West End these days. Now I find I've been stuck at the bottom. I just saw red and had to walk out. This is a matter of principal.

And Gracie, having been told what Dot had said in her rant to Harold Davison, boasted to the *London News Chronicle*:

> What did you say her name was? I've never heard of her either. Miss Squires is absolutely and indisputably wrong in saying that I am unknown. I made the big time when my recording of 'Butterfly' sold over one million copies in the United States. It sold well here too. I have made a movie and I've topped the bill in music-halls all over the States.

Dot's replacement for the Southampton show was Shirley Bassey, whilst the Broadway singer Fredye Marshall was brought in at the last minute for most of the other venues. Charlie Gracie, however, was the only one audiences were interested in. The comedy-impressionist Victor Seaforth recalled his performance supporting Gracie at the Glasgow Empire, hailed as "the artists' graveyard"—how the audience, likened to a rowdy football crowd, had chanted "Bugger off! Bring on Charlie Gracie!" all the way through his act. "It was the longest week of my life, and every performance was a nightmare," he remembered.

There was an interesting coda to the Charlie Gracie saga, when he turned up in the audience at one of Dot's shows at the Talk of the Town.

"He came on stage and gave me a hug," she recalled. "The audience were yelling for him to sing something, but he refused. I reacted kindly. I mean, I could hardly tell him to fuck off back to America in front of all those people, could I?"

At the end of 1957, Pye came up with the suggestion that Dot re-record twelve of Billy Reid's most celebrated songs, and release them on a vinyl album.

"I wanted Billy to do the arrangements and conduct the orchestra, but he wanted nothing to do with the idea or I guess with me," Dot said. "So they hired a bandleader I'd never heard of, and decided to throw in a few backing singers who completely buggered the whole thing up."

Dorothy Squires Sings Billy Reid came out the following year. Wielding the baton was British-born Bill Shepherd, unknown at the time. Later he worked with the likes of Joe Meek, Gene Vincent and Anthony Newley and in 1964 emigrated to Australia—where he was assigned to Festival

Records and began working with the Bees Gees, for which he will be best remembered. The backing singers denounced by Dot were the Beryl Stott Chorus, and to a certain extent she was right. High-powered numbers such as "Mother's Day", "I Still Believe" and "Safe In My Arms" were weakened by having someone crooning behind her, whilst "It's A Pity To Say Goodnight" was almost reduced to high-camp.

In January 1958 Dorothy and Moore made a lightning trip London where, over lunch in a Kensington restaurant, she gave an interview to John K Newnham of *TV Mirror & Disc News*. The feature was not published until two months later, and scotched the rumours—for now—that all was not well in the Squires household. The fact that Dot had given her husband explicit instructions to stay at their hotel and *not* attend the lunchtime interview should have provided a clue that their marriage was in trouble. Newnham asked where "Mr. Squires" was, and was told half-jokingly that this was not his concern. He observed:

> It's the marriage that people said could never last. The marriage of a singer who had been a star for many years to an unknown young actor. The marriage to a man over eight years her junior. But it *has* lasted. It will last. And you'd find it very difficult to find a happier couple than Roger Moore and Dorothy Squires.

Dot told Newnham that public opinion *had* affected her when she had first married Moore, a man much younger than herself, but for the benefit of the press she was content to keep up the charade and not let on that her marriage was falling apart:

I've never been so happy in my life, never so contented. I *did* feel embarrassed, though I hope I never showed it. Not embarrassed at having married him, but because so many people seemed to have doubts whether we could make a go of it, embarrassed in case Roger should feel embarrassed. But we both knew that it would turn out all right. We were, and still are, really in love. And he has been so good for me. I'm a different person. I was always a hothead, flaring up on the slightest provocation and upsetting myself. Roger is quiet and calm, and he has soothed out my temperament. He has cooled me down, quite deliberately but without making a fuss of doing so....I'm a much happier person because of this alone. I don't worry any more. It takes a lot to upset me. I can laugh off things that would have driven me crazy in the old days.

So, what *was* it that made Moore so special? Dot explained:

To start with he's got a wonderful sense of humour. That's a good basis for marriage. We laugh at the same things, and we laugh together a lot. He's affectionate and very sentimental. When we do quarrel, and all married couples have their disagreements, it is only over little things, and usually over other people and not about ourselves. And he never lets the quarrel last more than a few minutes. He just bursts into laughter, and it's all over and forgotten.

Newnham asked Dot how she and Moore had met, and her

story was a variant of what had actually happened: she had thrown a party at her home for Norman Newell, her recording manager, and her sister had called to ask if she could bring along a young man—this had been Roger Moore. Asked what her initial impression of him had been, she explained:

> To be absolutely truthful, I thought he was a bit of a bore. Strange how you can get the wrong impression of a person the first time, isn't it? Yet it's this very quietness of his that has since appealed to me so much. It just happened that we kept running into each other after that. I went along to the Palladium, and there he was with a bunch of my friends. Then we met again when I went along to the London Casino. He sent me a bottle of perfume for my birthday—and it broke in my case soon afterwards, making an awful mess of everything, and before we knew where we were in love, just like that!

Newnham wanted Dot's opinion of women marrying men younger than themselves. Her response was that she had it on good authority—from an American psychiatrist!—that the most successful Hollywood marriages were those where the wife was the older partner, and cited Rosalind Russell and Mary Pickford as examples. She went on:

> So much depends on the people concerned. It's not only that the wife should have the young outlook. The man has got to be mentally mature. Roger has always, ever since he was a boy, liked mixing with people older than himself. He was always mentally in advance of his own age. And he's always been a

home-lover and not a gadabout.

And Newnham's piece concluded:

> Dorothy and Roger have overcome all their first
> hurdles. They have confounded their critics. They
> have both found a deep, solid happiness and a
> perfect understanding. It's a marriage that shows
> every sign of lasting.

Moore *did* turn out to be a "gadabout" when, if the reports
in the press were true, he embarked on an affair with
Dorothy Provine, his co-star in ABC Television's *The
Alaskans*—an adventure series which takes place during
the 1890s Klondike Gold Rush, and his first regular work
on American television. Years later he denounced it as "my
most appalling television series ever." Provine (1935-2010)
later achieved fame for her role of Pinky Pinkham in *The
Roaring Twenties*. Dot told Anne de Courcy:

> I thought we had a super marriage. Wherever
> Roger was he would telephone twice a day and
> write letters. Of course I'd seen girls in shows
> running after stars so I knew what could happen.
> When a man like Roger goes on location there's
> always someone like that. But I used to think, 'What
> I don't know about is all right and won't hurt me.'"

Provine was still alive when Dot wrote her memoirs, and
what she has to say about her—and which would have had
to be heavily censored—is far from flattering. Yet at the
time she adds how she forgave Moore for straying from the
marital bed, and gives every impression that there were
times when she would have been content to share him with

someone else rather than lose him altogether. She recalls how he became moody and irritable, calling out the name Dorothy in his sleep, whereas he had always called *her* Dot. Therefore she asked him point-blank if he was having an affair with Provine, and he confessed that he was, and that he was infatuated with her. He then suggested that it might be a good idea if Dot flew back to England, where she was loved. She did, but a few weeks later returned to Hollywood upon being told that Moore had ended his affair with Provine. She writes of how he took her in his arms and begged her to forgive him. It was, she said, one of the most wonderful moments of her whole life, and she concludes this part of her story by claiming that the next two years had seen the two of them "gloriously happy".

She was stretching the truth, with her almost paranoid obsession with Moore clouding her judgement. Friends and acquaintances recalled public slanging matches when *The Alaskans* wrapped and the couple came back to Britain, rows which often became physically violent, with Dot doing all the bashing. In September 2012, the *Daily Mail*'s Glenys Roberts recalled turning up at Moore's home to interview him over lunch. By now he was with his third wife, and Roberts appears to have walked in on a domestic incident. Moreover, in their interview, and in a later television interview with Piers Morgan, Moore confessed to having been a victim of domestic violence, most especially where Dot had been concerned. One episode occurred, he said, as he had been nonchalantly plucking away at his guitar in order to *avoid* a confrontation:

> I was sitting on the edge of the table strumming and she was ranting on about something and I wasn't taking any notice. Next thing I know it was like slow motion, I could feel the guitar coming out of my hands and see it up above my head and bash, it came down. She ruined the guitar. She had a great temper.

Back in Hollywood the lavish parties continued, with the Moores entertaining movie royalty and putting on brave faces, hoping that they would sort out their difficulties, and with the neighbours still complaining about the noise. On 8 January, Dot learned that her friend Diana Dors and the new man in her life, Dickie Dawson, were in New York. She invited them to spend a few weeks at her home. She told me:

> Diana had the habit of always picking the wrong men. Her first husband started off by treating her like a rubbing rag and then used her as a punch-bag. The second one [Dawson] used her like a bank. Her last husband, Alan [Lake] was kind to her, but treated everybody else like shit. He spent time in prison for bashing someone. In between, there were dozens of lovers, hardly any of them worth writing home about.

A few years previously, Diana had been offered a Hollywood picture deal, on the proviso that her abusive, trouble-causing manager-husband Dennis Hamilton should not be allowed on the set. Obsessed with Burt Lancaster, who Diana said she was yearning to have an affair with, her dream had seemed close to achieving fruition when she had been offered a part opposite him, which Hamilton had rejected on her behalf. This had almost put paid to any chance of her having a Hollywood career, until she had gone over Hamilton's head and accepted a part in *The Unholy Wife*, during the shooting of which there had been a much-publicised affair with her leading man, Rod Steiger. Then had come an incident at the home of celebrity hairdresser, Raymond "Mr. Teasy-Weasy" Berrone, attended by many of Hollywood's glitterati, including Dot and Roger Moore. Hamilton had arranged a publicity stunt where Zsa Zsa Gabor was to be pushed into the pool, but when he and Diana were pushed in instead, he had belted

65

a photographer. The *National Enquirer*, covering the event, ran the headline, "Miss Dors Go Home, And Take Mr. Dors With You". Soon afterwards, Diana had announced her separation from this horribly aggressive man. Dot explained:

> She'd finally kicked her husband into touch and decided to leave him. The day before flying to New York, she went to see him and told him he'd never see him again. He told her, 'That's true, bitch, because by the time you get back here I'll be dead.' Her response to this was that she should be so lucky. Diana had a new man with her—he seemed smarmy to me, and she had no intention of ever being faithful to him. At one of my parties, I introduced her to Burt Lancaster. Later she told me that she'd already met him some years ago in London. 'He fucked me back then,' she said, "And he fucked me again after your party. It was great, catching up!"

It was Dot who took the call from England, on 31 January, that Dennis Hamilton had died a month earlier, the very day after Diana and Dawson had flown to New York. Hospitalised shortly after Diana had left for New York, he had succumbed to what was initially believed to have been a heart attack—it was tertiary syphilis. Dot told me:

> If I'd have been married to that man, I would have put poison in his tea. He was a louse, through and through. He treated Diana like something you'd scraped off the bottom of your shoe, yet she had nothing but praise for him after he died. It really was a case of good riddance to bad rubbish. Dennis Hamilton would sleep with anyone, male or female, next door's cat if it stood still long enough. I took the call. Diana thought it was him, again—he'd

66

been pestering her non-stop for two days—and she ran out of the room screaming she never wanted to talk to him again. I followed her upstairs and told her what happened, and she went to pieces. All of a sudden, the man she'd just called the most evil bastard in the world had become her lost knight in shining armour. She kept sobbing how Dennis was the only man she had ever loved—all very disconcerting for Dickie Dawson, who was standing next to her wondering what to do....

At the end of 1960 Dot was approached by the producer Ross Hunter, the doyenne of Hollywood's closeted gay movie community. Hunter (1926-76) specialised in frothy comedies such as *Pillow* Talk, and glossy melodramas like *Magnificent Obsession*, both starring his friend Rock Hudson. Hunter had an enormous penchant for gay-friendly stars like Doris Day, Debbie Reynolds, and Lana Turner. He was about to begin shooting *Tammy Tell Me True,* the second of the four *Tammy* films, with Sandra Dee and John Gavin, and having seen Dot many times on the stage commissioned her to compose the title-track. He was cautious—having been made aware of her unpredictable temper—to tell her that because she was not contracted to Universal Pictures *she* would not be allowed to perform the song over the soundtrack.

She recalled, "I told him, 'Who cares? I've been asked to contribute to a Hollywood film. That's good enough!'"

But, I wanted to know—had Sandra Dee interpreted the song to Dot's satisfaction?

Flat as a fart. She completely messed it up. Thank goodness Ruby Murray did a good version. I'd hate for my only film song to be remembered as done by

67

somebody who couldn't sing. Mind you, Ruby could be spectacularly off-key at times, especially when she'd had a tipple!

It *is* a beautiful song, but extant of the film sounds hammy and means nothing, which is why Dot never sang it in her concerts at the time—indeed, it was only ever performed once on stage. She recalled:

> There really was no place in the programme where I could comfortably fit it in. It certainly wouldn't have blended with the other songs in the Palladium shows. It wasn't in any way autobiographical, and I don't honestly think the fans were bothered about listening to it because unlike my other songs—even the ones I introduced just after the war—it very quickly dated.

Dot also declined to record in the studio until 1970, when it was included on her *Dorothy Sings Squires* album, but she said only as a last resort. Other cover-versions of the song were by Percy Faith (as part of the film soundtrack), future *Beverly Hillbillies* star Donna Douglas—and the Beatles, when their version, singing along to the original, was released in 1992 on their *Garage Tapes* album.

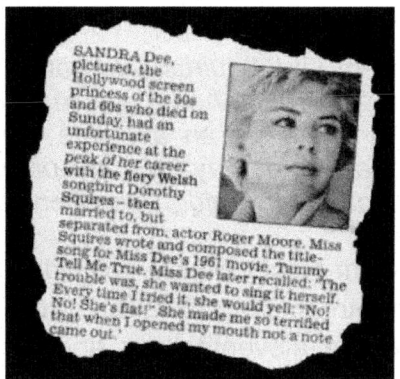

SANDRA Dee, pictured, the Hollywood screen princess of the 50s and 60s who died on Sunday, had an unfortunate experience at the peak of her career with the fiery Welsh songbird Dorothy Squires – then married to, but separated from, actor Roger Moore. Miss Squires wrote and composed the title-song for Miss Dee's 1961 movie, Tammy Tell Me True. Miss Dee later recalled: "The trouble was, she wanted to sing it herself. Every time I tried it, she would yell: "No! No! She's flat!" She made me so terrified that when I opened my mouth not a note came out."

Dot disliked Sandra Dee,
and the feeling was mutual

Hollywood, 1961, with a "starlet" fan

5: Where Can I Go?

"Working with Dorothy Squires alternated between bliss and sheer insanity. On one hand she was the consummate professional, on the other an absolute martinet if things weren't done exactly her way. Would I put myself through all that again? You bet I would!" Russ Conway.

The final split from Roger Moore coincided with a concert at London's Metropolitan Theatre, when Dot's pianist dropped out at the eleventh hour and the management brought in Russ Conway. She recalled:

> That man was too beautiful to be true. I think I fell head-over-heels in love with him the moment we met. But, it was not to be. Russ was such a lovely man, but he was very troubled, always a bag of nerves because he was terrified of the world finding out that he was gay, and he had a partner. Most of his fans were women who were besotted with him. Had his secret become public knowledge, it would have ended his career. This was why he was so ill much of the time with his nerves, why he smoked like a chimney and suffered from ulcers.

The partner was Liverpool-born singer Michael Holliday, who topped the UK charts in 1958 with one of Bacharach and David's earliest compositions, "The Story of My Life". Neurotic, and unable to cope with his demons, Holliday took his own life in October 1963, aged thirty-eight.

Born Trevor Stanford in Bristol, in September 1925, Russ Conway was as psychologically damaged as he was

70

indeed handsome. A rebellious youth, he had taught himself to play the piano whilst serving three years in a young offenders institution and, in the hope of calming him down, in 1942 his father had pushed him into joining the Merchant Navy, where he had worked as a signalman on minesweepers, a dangerous profession for which he had been awarded the Distinguished Service Medal. Whilst with the Navy, he had developed a propensity towards being accident prone—in the first of many mishaps, he lost the tip of the third finger of his right hand whilst using a bread-slicer. In 1948, he was discharged from military service after developing a stomach ulcer, and not long afterwards began playing the piano in clubs in and around London. As Trevor Stanford, he was spotted by an EMI talent scout, and hired by the studio as a backing musician, accompanying Gracie Fields, Dennis Lotis, and Joan Regan who became a lifelong friend.

Conway's "honky-tonk" style was so distinctive that Columbia encouraged him to record a single. "Party Pops", a medley of standards, was released in 1957 and entered the Top 30. Between then and working with Dot he enjoyed six Top Ten albums and fourteen Top 30 hits and sold 30 million records, with the self-composed "Sidesaddle" and "Roulette" topping the charts, the latter dethroning Elvis Presley's "A Fool Such As I". Like Dot's "Mother's Day" it ended up on the jukebox at Graceland.

Conway did not mind being compared with the other piano great of the day, Winifred Atwell, but hated being labelled "the British Liberace". Glamorous he may have been but he was never over-the-top camp. He dressed soberly on stage and though an aficionado of expensive cars he did not live a flamboyant lifestyle, declaring that he never wanted to lose touch with his humble roots.

In the wake of the *Dorothy Squires Sings Billy Reid* album—and, she said, peeved with the company for "forcing" her to work with a backing group and an orchestra leader she had never heard of until arriving at the studio—Dot had left Pye and signed with Columbia. Her debut single, Rodgers and Hart's "Bewitched", coupled with her own composition "A Secret That's Never Been Told" failed to make much of an impression, likewise its successor, "This Place Called Home". With her next venture, she hit the jackpot.

Dot had written "Say It With Flowers" after completing her album of Billy Reid songs, her idea being that her next album should have a flowers theme. Pye had not been interested, however, and she had placed the handwritten sheet music in the piano stool at her Hollywood home and forgotten about it. According to one story, Dot threw a party one evening where the guests included Norman Newell and Russ Conway—who, whilst Dot was in the kitchen preparing cocktails rummaged around in Dot's piano stool, found "Say It With Flowers", and began playing it, bringing the comment from its composer that the song sounded vaguely familiar.

"Absolute bullshit," she recalled. "Russ was at the party, of course, but I was already performing the song, though not the way I sang it on the record. That particular arrangement came about purely by chance when my orchestra leader at the time, Tony Osborne, brought in Russ Conway for the London show when my regular pianist fell ill."

On stage at the Metropolitan Theatre, Dot was unprepared for Conway's embellishments halfway through the song, and found herself singing the last two stanzas an octave higher. The "new", big-belter Dorothy Squires had been born!

"It was easier hitting the top notes than singing them soft and low," she said. "I realised that I could let myself go without going off-key, so I rewrote the arrangement."

"Say It With Flowers" is the first truly magnificent Squires *chanson-réaliste*, more so than anything she ever did with Billy Reid in that it is entirely her own creation—lyrics, music and arrangement. Her delivery and Russ Conway's introduction and piano solo middle section are eclectic and send shivers down the spine. Accompanied by Tony Osborne's orchestra, they recorded the song in a single take on 19 May 1961, coupled with Dot's reworking of the Fred Weatherley-Haydn Wood World War I favourite, "Roses of Picardy", written in 1916 and introduced by the American musical-comedy star Harry Pilcer. He and others who had popularised the song, including John McCormack, had sung the verses recounting the sad tale of "Colinette with the sea-blue eyes", who waits in vain by the roadside for her lost love, whilst the wind blowing through the poplar trees murmurs their favourite song. Dot considered this "old hat" and sang only the verse and repeated the refrain, but with such effect and precision that her version of the song becomes definitive. The single peaked at Number 23 in the hit-parade and remained in the charts for ten weeks, her first hit parade success since "I'm Walking Behind You", eight years earlier. Dot and Conway performed the song—to the animals—during a televised episode of *Billy Smart's Circus*, at around the time she started a precedent for suing people, sometimes for ludicrous reasons. In this instance, she brought in her lawyer when David Jacobs played the record on the BBC's top-rating *Juke Box Jury*—and erroneously introduced her as *Rosemary* Squires, a popular songstress of the day. Wisely, the lawyer talked her out of taking legal action against the BBC, warning her that if she did, she might never appear on television again!

The record's success led to Bernard Delfont breaking his own rules and engaging Dot for a season at London's Talk of the Town, the former Hippodrome Theatre acquired by him in 1958 and transformed into a nightclub. Until now,

Delfont had only contracted big American entertainers such as Sammy Davis Jr, Eartha Kitt, and Lena Horne. To her chagrin, Dot did not have to deal with Delfont himself but was "saddled" with his deputy, Robert Nesbitt, a somewhat pompous individual who at the time was also responsible for staging the Royal Variety Show. An unpleasant spat between Dot and Nesbitt was recalled by his assistant, Rosalyn Wilder, in the autumn issue of *Call Boy*, the official publication of the British Music Hall Society:

> The scene is the Talk of the Town, late on Monday afternoon. Dorothy Squires is opening that night as the headline cabaret. Mr. Nesbitt has spent the afternoon lighting her act. He clearly is not happy and he goes up to her, puts his arm around her and says, "Dorothy, darling. I really don't think that song is the right choice for the act." "Well," flounces Miss Squires. "I don't care what you think, it stays in." More persuasion from Mr. N, more stubborn behaviour from the star. "Well, darling," says Mr. Nesbitt. "If you really must sing it, I suggest you sing it in the taxi on the way home."

Wilder does not mention the title of song, which Dot had told me about some years earlier:

> The song was "The Talk of the Town", which I found appropriate, seeing as that's where I was singing. But the snooty bugger wasn't having it. "It's a song about scandal, not about this theatre," he said. "I'm *ordering* you to leave it out!" I promised that I would, then sang it to open the show. It brought the house down!

Nesbitt would have his revenge. Dot had been pencilled in for the 1962 Royal Variety Show scheduled for April, which would have seen her sharing the bill with Rosemary Clooney and Sophie Tucker. Bernard Delfont subsequently crossed her name off the list.

Dot and Russ Conway would enter the studio for a second time in January 1962 to record "Talk It Over With Someone", Norman Newell's adaptation of a German song composed by Werner Sharfenberger—whose "Sailor" he had also adapted, giving Petula Clark a number one hit. For some reason, Columbia prevented Conway from accompanying her on the B-side—Dave Coleman's "Blue Snowfall", a dreary piece which subsequently became the A-side. Dot maintained that this was the reason it did not chart like its predecessor, because disc jockeys refused to play it.

In the meantime, Dot's marriage reached crisis point when in July 1961 she began to suspect that Roger Moore may have been cheating on her. The emotion—indeed, this might almost be described as paranoia, if not psychosis—was still there when she wrote about it sixteen years later. Moore had been in Zagreb (then in Yugoslavia) filming the locations for *Il ratto delle Sabine* (UK: *Romulus and the Sabines*), a hammy sword-and-sandal adventure directed by Richard Pottier, of which the least said the better. He had promised to be home in time to celebrate their eighth wedding anniversary, and she was lying next to the pool when he called her to announce that he had just arrived at London airport. It was the first time, she says, that she had never been at an airport to meet him, and this set off the alarm bells. Then when he arrived at St Mary's Mount, instead of sweeping her up into his arms as he usually did, he paid the taxi driver, virtually ignored her, went into the house and placed his luggage in the spare room. Later, they drove to his mother's home, and Moore announced that he would be leaving for Rome the next morning, where more locations were to be shot, and asked Dot to accompany him. One gets the impression that if he *had* been seeing someone else he was feeling rueful about the whole thing, and wanted Dot with him to ensure that it would not happen again. She, however, had a radio broadcast the next day, and promised to catch up with him later in the week. Then she asked him if he had met anyone in Zagreb, and he affirmed that he had—Marshal Tito. At this, she says, she went berserk, screaming and awakening the household, then rushing out into the night and driving home.

The drama resumed when Dot arrived at Moore's hotel, in Rome. It was almost midnight and he had left a note with the desk clerk saying that he was unable to meet her because the director had ordered a last-minute early shoot, therefore he would be sleeping on the lot. Dot assumed this must have been some distance out of Rome, but when told that it was just twenty miles away, again her suspicions were aroused. The couple met, Dot hung around the set until Moore had finished filming, and that night they went out dancing. They argued furiously when he told her that he had arranged to pay his $44,000 fee for the film into *her* bank account. The next day Dot returned to London, assuming that Moore intended reimbursing her with the money she had doled out on him over the years whilst helping him launch his career—because he had decided that it was time to move on.

The couple made up briefly when Moore took a short break from filming and flew home. However, once the film wrapped and he returned to Bexley, he began sleeping in the spare room, and soon afterwards was hospitalised with a kidney complaint. It was at this point that Moore's physician—she names him in her memoirs as Dr Plunkett—took her lunch and breaking doctor-patient confidentiality rules told her that Moore had been seeing another woman in Zagreb. Even more astonishing is her admission that Plunkett agreed to be with her for moral support at Moore's bedside when she confronted him about his affair—which he admitted, suggesting that she too should have one so that they would be even.

Moore moved out of St Mary's Mount, and he and Dot did not see each other for eight months, when he showed up at Bexley having learned that his father-in-law, Archie Squires, was terminally ill. Her father's death was but part of a double blow for Dot, who at the same time was made aware of the identity of Moore's mistress: Luisa Mattioli, an Italian who had played the second female lead in *Il ratto delle Sabine*.

"The only thing going through my confused mind when I found out was revenge," she told me. "I wanted to kill her—in fact, I wanted to kill her twice because I was sure back then that she had led him on. Now, of course, I know differently."

Dot took the most unusual step of suing Moore for "loss of conjugal rights". When he refused the court order to return to her within 28 days, she tracked him down to the house he and Luisa were renting and got her secretary, Hilda, to drive her there late at night after coming off stage, saying that she was too tired to drive there herself and promising there would be no trouble. When she arrived at the house, she went out of control—confessing in her memoirs that loving someone *so* much had this effect on her. Parked outside were the "his and hers" cars—Moore's Alvis and Luisa's Volkswagen. Looking through the window she saw two cups and saucers on the table. Finding the door locked, she took off her shoe and smashed the glass with her heel. Then, she says, she suffered temporary amnesia from which she emerged whilst sitting in her bath, back home, with lacerations on her wrists, arms and legs.

It subsequently emerged that when the police had arrived, Dot had screamed at one of them, "Give me a leg up to the window, Sarge, I'm about to kill me an Italian!" The press also reported that, whilst one of the other officers had been trying to cuff her, Dot had broken free, grabbed Moore's sweater and rent it in two, wiped the blood down his chest and yelled, "Here's my blood. Take it. You've taken everything else!", to which Moore responded,

"Take her to the nearest nut-house and put her in a strait-jacket."

Neither Moore nor Luisa pressed charges against Dot, and she later claimed that she *had* offered him a divorce, providing he paid her a cash settlement of £5,000. Moore was not a yet a big name, and when he informed her that he did not have that kind of money to spare, he was speaking the truth—whilst Dot was exceedingly wealthy. The only conclusion to be reached is that, *knowing* only too well that he could not afford to pay her, Dot was hoping that Moore would see sense, ditch Luisa, and return to her as per the instructions of the court order. This did not happen.

Dot said in her final television interview that she had stopped loving Roger Moore when she had stopped respecting him, but this was untrue. Over the years, she *never* bad-mouthed him so far as I am aware, and she never stopped respecting him. Likewise Moore, who supported her—morally and often financially—until the end of her life. In his memoirs he writes that he was not proud of the way their marriage had ended and deeply regrets any heartache he caused. He concludes:

> I didn't then realise it, but the long separations in the pursuit of our individual careers had obviously had an impact on me, on us both, perhaps. We had, quite simply, drifted apart without realising what was happening. I never stopped caring about Dot. I don't think you can ever stop caring about someone who was such a large part of your life, no matter how your relationship has ended. I don't think she ever stopped caring about me, either…

If any good did come out of the situation it was that Dot wrote a lengthy, harrowing song about her feelings, now that she was aware that Moore was out of her life for good. In "Where Can I Go?" she asks, where can she *go* without him, how can she *live* without him, where she can find a corner to hide and handle with care a heart that just died? She knows that she must walk on and find a place in the sun, but concludes that this will be impossible—for wherever she goes and whatever she does, she will still see his face. It was the first of many songs wherein she lamented her lost love, though she would try to fob off journalists with the excuse that their content was purely coincidental. As had happened with Edith Piaf when the great love of her life, the boxer Marcel Cerdan, had been killed in a plane crash, Dot *never* got over Roger Moore, her reactions frequently giving one the impression that he had actually died. I only heard her sing "Where Can I Go" once on stage, and it was an almost unbearable experience. Indeed, it was as if she actually enjoyed putting herself through all the unnecessary pain and anguish when she was well aware that she was never going to get him back.

After the split from Moore, Dot's name was romantically linked with several men brought along as guests to her parties which raged on, as if nothing had happened. All of these were gay. One was female impersonator Danny La Rue, another was an internationally-renowned pop star, still with us at the time of writing, a third the footballer Derek Dougan. All three turned up at her home and later at her concerts, with male partners. Her unlikeliest "suitor" was without any doubt future prime minister Edward Heath. Around the same age as Dot, they had first met in 1950 when Heath had been elected Conservative MP for Bexley, since which time they had become friends, going out on "dates" and sharing intimate dinners. Because this never came up in conversation, I never got around to asking Dot if their relationship had progressed beyond the platonic, but given Heath's "permanent bachelor status" one may assume not. It was only after his death in July 2005 that the general public learned of his friendship with Dot, when her former secretary, Hilda Diaz, told the *Daily Express*:

They became extremely close friends and were on easy and affectionate terms with each other...[Heath] sometimes used her house and its extensive grounds for charity events. He and Dot opened several fetes in the Bexley area and became extremely fond of each other. Ted was not a shy man, and contrary to what people say, did have a sense of humour, although he was always somewhat defensive where women were concerned...Dot and Ted used to go out socially and on one occasion I said. "You ought to marry Dot. You make a lovely couple and get on so well." Ted thought about this for a moment and began to laugh. Dot could be a fiery character, and was always referring to Luisa as "the bloody Italian". "Marry Dot?" said Ted. "That's quite an idea. But if I did, I think we'd be at war with Italy within six weeks!"

Over the next four years Dot recorded twelve songs under her Columbia contract. Released on six singles they sold well but not in sufficient quantities to chart. Nine were self-composed or collaborations with Ernie Dunstall, and reflected her mixed up private life. "Someone Other Than Me" was in a class of its own, as was her stunning arrangement of Edwin Lemare's "Moonlight And Roses" which had started life as *Andantino in D-flat* for organ in 1888, and not given lyrics until 1921.

On 7 January 1963, Dot was Roy Plomley's guest on BBC Radio's *Desert Island Discs*. The records she selected to take with her to the imaginary island were not what her fans might have expected: Tony Osborne's "Secrets Of The Seine", her recording of "Roses Of Picardy", Debussy's *Clair de lune*, Billy Cotton Band Show regular vocalist Kathie Kay singing "Till Tomorrow", instrumental pieces by Edmundo Ros and trumpeter Eddie Calvert—and Percy Faith's Orchestra playing "Tammy Tell

Me True". For her "Castaway's Favourite" she chose Russ Conway's *Concerto for Dreamers*, and her book choice was Vaughan Haddock's *Book of Modern Verse*. For her luxury item, she chose a piano.

Over the next eighteen months there were sell-out shows up and down the country, but only two singles were released by Columbia in 1963, with three of the four songs written by Dot. "Bless Your Heart My Darling" was considered so old-fashioned that it received virtually no airplay—likewise its successor, "I Won't Cry Anymore", though the flipside, "Red the Rose", was exceptional and always well-received in her shows. Her only single of 1964, a collaboration with Ernie Dunstall, was "Look Around". In the November of this year, Dunstall presented her with "Where In The World?" a dramatic piece which she deliberated over for a week before "launching" it at one of her parties, performing it *a cappella* for her guests:

> *Where in the world will I find another shoulder to cry on, another heart to rely on, now you're gone?*
> *Where in the world will I find love, if there's no future around the bend?*

One of the party guests was Kathy Kirby. Dot recalled:

> Kathy and I had much in common. Both of us had started out with famous bandleaders—older men who had treated us like shit. In Kathy's case, her man was still treating her like shit, and would do so until the day he died. I finished singing the song, and she burst into tears. I gave her the sheet music, and when she dropped by a few days later and sang it to me, I realised that I would never do it so well, so I gave the song to her. It was the best thing she ever did.

Kathy had been discovered by bandleader Bert Ambrose—

forty-four years her senior. Domineering and aggressive, she stayed with him long after their relationship ended, and he remained her Svengali until his death in 1971, after which time her career entered a downward spiral from which it never recovered. Dot never recorded "Where In The World?" but she did sing it occasionally on stage.

Meanwhile, unhappy with the way Columbia was handling her record releases, Dot negotiated a deal with Decca. When the executives here told her how much they had loved "Say It With Flowers" she declared that from now on she would sing *only* her own compositions. As a songwriter-composer she was remarkably astute, keeping the lyrics simple but effective, and the melodies uncomplicated. Her first recordings for Decca—"Goodbye", and "Have I Waited Too Long", collaborations with Ernie Dunstall—were not what the company was looking for, but they put them out on a single to please her hoping that it would enjoy the same success as "Say It With Flowers". When this flopped she was coerced into recording Joe Lubin's "Evermore", which was not what *she* was looking for. She therefore threw in the towel with Decca, who subsequently held her to the terms of her contract, declaring that she still owed them an album. Dot said that she would come up with twelve standards, and it was agreed that she and Ernie Dunstall would do the arrangements. In the meantime, the lavish parties continued at her Bexley home. Marion Montgomery, the American jazz singer and our mutual friend who moved to England in 1965, recalled:

> Dorothy—I *never* called her Dot—had an open-house policy. Really, she was too generous for her own good, which was why so many people used her. When you attended one of her parties you were flung into a veritable A to Z of celebrities from all walks of life—movie stars, actors, singers, musicians. Once when I was there, this odd-looking

little man kept staring at me from where he was sitting all alone in a corner of the room, and I asked Dorothy who he was. She shrugged her shoulders and responded, "How the bloody hell should I know? He's been here for the past three days but he appears to be having a good time. He's even helped out once or twice in the kitchen." It turned out that he had come to fix a problem with the pool.

And courtesy of one of these parties, another "great love" had entered Dot's life, or so she tried to convince herself:

I really did think he was the one. It just shows how wrong you can sometimes be! On the positive side, though, once the ardour cooled we *did* remain friends and I would like to think that some of my better songs came about as a result of our collaborations together.

Dot as Ann Hart in *Stars in Your Eyes* (1956), with her
leading man, Bonar Colleano. She was devastated
when he was killed in a car crash, aged 34.

Publicity shot for Columbia Records, 1962.

Partying at St Mary's Mount with Russ Conway
and Cliff Richard, c.1963

Dot and Russ Conway (right), sampling smoked
herrings in Arbroath, Scotland, c.1964.

Dot outside the High Court in 1962 for the divorce
hearing with Roger Moore. She said, "The Italian
wasn't the only one who could look stylish!"

6: Point Of No Return

"With a characteristic outburst of undiluted expletives, she's always managed to gird her loins and storm back at the world with ferocious determination." Tony Stewart.

The new man in Dot's life was 36-year-old actor Mark Eden, currently appearing in the television drama series, *Catch Hand*. Best described as a precursor to *Auf Wiedersehen Pet*, this told of the adventures of a pair of "Jack-the-lad" construction workers—Eden's co-star was Anthony Booth, who later played the rapscallion son-in-law in *Till Death Us Do Part*—who travel the country in search of work, but spend much of their time chasing girls. Eden is best remembered for portraying creepy Alan Bradley in *Coronation Street*. In his autobiography he is somewhat unkind when remembering Dot. He claims that they first met when she dropped in at a mutual friend's house, and that she invited him to one of her parties. He adds:

> I still can't remember how she and I ended up in bed that night, but we did and a bizarre kind of relationship began. From the start it was an unlikely liaison. Dot was 18 years older than me [sic] and not the kind of woman I normally found attractive. She was loud and brash, wore chunky, ostentatious jewellery, drove a Ford Thunderbird, and swore like a Billingsgate porter...We seemed to hit it off, in a macabre kind of way. To describe our subsequent affair as tempestuous would be an understatement. We both had explosive tempers allied to short fuses, and we had constant pyrotechnical rows.

As with Roger Moore, Dot never bad-mouthed Mark Eden and always spoke of him with great fondness. She remembered:

I needed to get away from England. I was hurting after the split from Roger, so I decided to take a trip to the Costa del Sol with the first man I met, and I took Alan and Ernie [Dunstall] with me. A couple of gay friends knew someone who could rent us a villa in Torremolinos—a little place back then, as compared to the sprawling metropolis of today. The holiday was a disaster.

According to Eden, there were rows because Dot wanted to laze in the sunshine all day, whilst he and the others wanted to explore the surrounding area.

"I left them to their own devices," she said. "Lying on the beach gave me time to think and take stock of my life."

Like most of her men, Eden cheated on Dot. His first wife was Joan Malin—they divorced in 1959, and she later married John le Mesurier, after his divorce from Hattie Jacques.

"I knew he was cheating on me," Dot confessed. "I knew when *all* of them cheated on me. Most of them were nobodies when they got to know me. They used me for what they could get out of me, then they moved on. Mark was no different."

Her musical director Nicky Welsh was scathing of the way Dot was treated by those she helped, and was often there to offer a friendly shoulder to lean upon:

First off there was Billy Reid, a big name when Dot met him, and who became bigger after working with her. Then there was Roger Moore. Had it not been for Dot, he would have still been posing for those knitting patterns. Then there was the bloke from *Coronation Street*. All of them were there for the hand-outs, and only Roger had anything decent to say about Dot behind her back. They treated her like shit—and the worst thing of all was that she let

89

them treat her like shit. Where men were concerned, she was the biggest sucker in the business.

With Mark Eden, Dot developed a project—*Old Rowley*, more of which later, was a musical comedy-drama which takes place at the court of King Charles II.

On 24 March 1965, Eden opened in Tennessee Williams' *The Night of the Iguana* at London's Savoy Theatre. His co-star was Sian Phillips, who Dot looked forward to meeting at the after-show party. She was not invited, however, having been told by Eden that this was for cast-members only. What she did not know was that he was seeing one of the cast members—27-year-old Patricia Shakesby—behind her back. Dot was suspicious—but there was no way, she said, that she would be attending the premiere to be sent home afterwards and miss the party. Eden observes in his autobiography of how she "went berserk" when he told her—over the phone, rather than to her face—about Shakesby. She called him incessantly, he adds, becoming such a nuisance that he had to take the receiver of the hook to get a good night's sleep.

Revenge was sweet when Dot called Eden from the studio and invited him for a drink "for old times' sake". The evening apparently went well until Dot offered to drive him home. No sooner had he got into her Ford Thunderbird than she locked all doors and slammed her foot down on the accelerator and announced that this time, *she* was taking *him* for ride. Eden observes how she drove like a maniac across South London, taking corners on two wheels, jumping traffic lights, until they were out in the country, where she stopped the car and made him get out, leaving him stranded in the middle of nowhere.

Eden concludes, "To paraphrase Congreve: "Heaven has no rage like love to hatred turned. Nor Hell nor fury like Dot Squires scorned."

Dot was the first to admit that she could be difficult and unpredictable, and that this prevented some men from wanting to get involved with her. She told Sally Clyde:

> I know I can't change my ego, in or out of show business. But when my head gets as big as a mountain, I try to keep my feet on the ground. I know I frighten some people. It sometimes happens in my love life. But I'm terribly feminine, really. Sex is no problem except I'm one of those people who have to be in love for it to be good. I envy the dame who can just jump in the sack. She can't ever be hurt.

Dot and Mark Eden appear to have made up their differences when, on 6 December 1966, he, Ernie Dunstall and Decca's Michael Barclay accompanied her to Llanelli—her first visit to the town of her birth in sixteen years—for three concerts at the Regal Cinema, where she had watched *The Jazz Singer* as a child and dreamed of becoming an entertainer herself.

In retrospect these autobiographical performances heralded what may be described as Dot's secondary career as a gifted and astute *chanteuse-entrepreneuse*. Not only had she personally hired the hall and organised the lighting and supervised the sound-system, she had persuaded Decca to record each concert, so that she and they could choose the best one to be released on the album she owed them. She reflected:

> I was fed up of people ordering me around—telling me what to sing, how to sing it. The way I saw things, it was my voice that I was flogging, therefore from now on I would be doing things my way. The big boss man at Decca protested, saying as how he wanted his twelve standards. So I said, 'Fine. If that

is what you want, then you'd better sing them your bloody self!

Decca reacted by assigning Dot to their budget label, Ace of Clubs. The Llanelli shows were organised in such a hurry that there was no time to print playbills—therefore armed with a large sheet of paper and a roll of Cellotape, Dot made her own and stuck it on the entrance to the cinema. Much was made of her arrival in the town, and she was filmed by a local news magazine visiting friends and relatives she had not seen in years—and inspecting her playbill before barging straight past a group of excited reporters, completely ignoring them and getting into her car. She did later speak briefly to one, but only to enthuse about *Old Rowley*, saying that she and Mark Eden had now composed seventeen songs for the £125,000 production, which was scheduled to open in January 1967, after which she planned returning to the United States for an extended tour.

So, *what* exactly was *Old Rowley* about? Dot wrote a great deal about it in her memoirs. She had, she said, researched her subject for many years and the message of the play had been to explain the reasons for Charles II's sexual pranks. Nell Gwynn, she added, may have been his most famous mistress but she was by no means his only one, and all of them had been accepted by his queen, Catherine of Braganza. She concluded that it had always been her intention to have Paul Schofield playing the randy king, and cast herself in the role of Nell Gwynn.

Decca agreed with Dot that the best of the three Llanelli concerts was the final one, recorded on 8 October, because after singing her closing number she walked back on to the stage and led the audience in a raucous but intensely moving unrehearsed singalong which included "Back In Your Own Backyard"—the title she had chosen for the album, but which was later changed to *This Is My Life!*

—and the Welsh favourite, "We'll Keep A Welcome In The Hillside". What is sad, from a fan's point of view, was that though the show lasted two hours, only 43 minutes of it ended up on the album and the discarded songs were assigned to a Decca vault. These included "Someone Other Than Me", "Look Around"…and "Say It With Flowers". Compared to her later, legendary live albums, this one is primitive—badly recorded and edited, off-stage noises, microphone "pops"—yet it is almost as important because it set a precedent. Dorothy Squires *always* gave more exemplary performances in front of audiences as opposed to in the studio. She told me:

> On stage, you only get one chance. Fuck it up, and they boo you. This is why most of my studio recordings were put down with one take. Maybe some of them might have sounded better with a second take, but that's not what professionalism is about. On stage there are never any second takes.

As yet there was no "signature tune", and wearing a purple diaphanous gown trimmed with feathers she opened with Anthony Newley and Leslie Bricusse's "On A Wonderful Day Like Today". This ran into her "Once Upon A Time There Was a Little Girl" sequence where she told how Nenna became Dorothy: of her trip to London, her failed auditions, her tribulations and redemption courtesy of Billy Reid. She recalls her time in America and the songs she sang here, and inevitably her failed marriage—the songs are "Yesterday" and "When You Lose the One You Love"—but there is some hope for a brighter future when she closes with "Everything's Coming Up Roses".

Ever the perfectionist, Dot was not happy with the way the recording engineers "fucked up" her first live album, though at the time she was only grateful that Decca had allowed her to make it in the first place. In 1972, when it was re-released by Jay Boy Records, she had her say:

The incidents I sing about really happened, but it's hardly "my life" as it only briefly touches this life of mine, and being a single LP, there was so much edited out. Even though it was my money that financed the venture, I wasn't consulted about its release date, what was to be left in or what was to be taken out. I was lucky to be getting it released. The fact that one has a name doesn't mean that one sells records, and at the time I recorded this album I wasn't selling records. In fact, I didn't have much incentive as my life didn't matter very much to me then, and like thousands of others mortals my marriage was over, so I didn't care if I sang, lived or died.

Poor the album may have been, though through no fault of its perfectionist star it nevertheless opened the gates of one of the most glittering—and controversial—secondary careers in British show business history. Jay Boy was a subsidiary of President Records, the New York independent label, founded by Edward Kassner in 1955—the British arm of the company was established two years later, when many of Kassner's US hits were licensed out to Decca. His big scoop, and one which earned him a fortune, was in buying the rights to the song "Rock Around The Clock" for just $250. Kassner (1920-96) had seen Dot several times on stage in America, and added her name to his varied catalogue of stars which included Felice Taylor, Barry White, The Equals who topped the charts with "Baby Come Back", Viola Wills—and Charlie Gracie.

"Eddie Kassner wanted me to do a show with Gracie, and said something about it being for old times' sake and an exercise in building bridges," she remembered. "I told him, 'Fuck that for a bowl of soup!'"

In 1968, Dot cut three singles with President. Five of the six songs were self-composed. "When There's Love In Your Heart" champions the precognitive dream—the belief that all will turn out fine so long as this is what one wishes. It was backed with the powerful "Where Can I Go?" A new version of "Roses of Picardy" appeared on the B-side of "Point of No Return", in which Dot attempts to cope with losing the great love of her life by pretending the split never happened. "Your Flowers Arrived Too Late" also deals with lost love, but in this instance it is Dot who is telling the story: she is at a friend's house when the friend's lover drops by, hoping to make amends after a quarrel—only to discover that it is too late because the woman has left without saying goodbye. It was backed with "Red the Rose", and received more airplay on the BBC than any previous Dorothy Squires song.

Each single sold well, and though none reached the Top 50, if one compares sales numbers then with today, the 150,000 copies sold of "Your Flowers Arrived Too Late" would have seen it reaching the Top Ten. The executives at President were content with the way things were going with Dot, and when she told them of her dream to release an album with a flowers theme, they told her to go ahead—so long as this contained a mixture of her compositions *and* well-established standards.

Scots-born Nicky Welsh was brought in to produce, do the arrangements and conduct the orchestra. And what a musical genius this man was! So hilariously funny, too. Only he could get away with splitting a word in two to add the word "fuck", and *never* sound in the slightest offensive! Prior to working with Dot—whom he regarded as the most important person he *ever* worked with—his favourite artiste, he told me, had been Cilla Black, having arranged her versions of "Yesterday" and "Don't Answer Me" besides most of the tracks on her best-selling album, *Cilla Sings A Rainbow*. He recalled:

> It was the beginning of a friendship made in heaven. Dot and I had the same ideas and the same temperament. We got along, just like a house

95

on fire from the moment we met. Sometimes there would be the odd, nonsensical little outburst such as when we'd put down 'Tulips from Amsterdam' and Dot shouted "Fuck!" twenty times. I asked her why she'd done that and she replied, "You've said *fuck* more times that I have today, boyo. Now we're even!" Thenon it was always referred to as "The Fuck Song". But to work with, perhaps more than anyone else, she was an absolute perfectionist. The one thing that Cilla Black had in common with Dorothy Squires was that both were always surrounded by queens. So if you saw [Cilla] out with a guy, no matter who he was, he'd inadvertently let the cat out of the bag. And Cilla's husband [Bobby Willis] was intensely homophobic, which was confusing to say the least. You never got that with the straight men in Dot's entourage. Cilla was tremendous to work with, but like Dot such a consummate professional that you forgot the tantrums and just got on with it.

The album opens with "Say It With Flowers", and ends with its reprise. Between, Dot takes us on a roller-coaster of emotion, initially not too dramatic as she breezes through "I'll Be With You in Apple Blossom Time" before offering a near-definitive reading of Ivor Novello's "We'll Gather Lilacs". "Moonlight And Roses" and "Roses of Picardy", sandwiched on each side of "Honeysuckle Rose", are even more powerful than Dot's earlier recordings of these songs. Side Two opens with "Your Flowers Arrived Too Late", after which comes light relief with "Tulips from Amsterdam". Next up is "When the Poppies Bloom Again", thirty-two years after Dot crooned this as a band singer. Astonishing does not begin to describe this reworked version, declared by some critics as the best song on the album. Then comes the bouncy "I'm Looking Over A Four-Leaf Clover"—before Dot rounds off the proceedings with "Red the Rose" and her own "Our Garden" in which she laments her failed marriage. Magnificent!

Dot saw red in 1968 when the actor Kenneth More jokingly remarked during a live televised BAFTA ceremony that his friend Roger Moore's "wife" was more attractive than he was. ITV broadcast an apology, but this did not prevent Dot from suing the actor *and* the channel. More observed:

> The evening seemed to pass off splendidly. But within a few weeks I received a letter from a firm of solicitors claiming that I had slandered their client, Miss Dorothy Squires, who was in fact Mrs. Roger Moore, in that I had called another woman his wife. At that time Louisa was not married to Roger, although she had borne him two children. I knew that he had been married to Dorothy Squires, but so far as the world was concerned, he was living with Luisa as his wife...I wrote a letter of apology, but the solicitors replied this was not sufficient. Dorothy Squires was going to sue me in the High Court. I therefore consulted my old friend, Michael Havers [later the Attorney General who declared Dot a vexatious litigant]. The jury took thirty minutes to decide what I had said was not defamatory...

The failed libel action convinced Dot she had made Moore wait too long for his divorce, believing he would return to her once he tired of Luisa. Now, he was granted his freedom. Dot told Sally Clyde that had it not been for the break-up she would not have forged ahead with her career:

> When Roger left me, I felt a misery impossible to imagine. My only brother had just died. My father died right at that time. I'll never know how I took it all, those endless nights when I walked these grounds, alone. I read by day and I walked by night.

I knew even then that I couldn't change things, that Roger and I wouldn't get back together. But he gave me the courage to change my status in show business. I was able to do this because I wasn't an ordinary housewife. When I lost one person, I was able to find compensation in hundreds thousands... my public.

She told Margaret Pride, of *Reveille*:

The break-up of my marriage put a steel rod right through my back. I determined I would never again suffer such agonies as I did then. To the world I presented a tough, aggressive front. I have always done my weeping in private. And there was plenty of that. I was so shattered.

In April 1969, Roger Moore and Luisa Mattioli—who in the seven years they had been together now had two children, were married. With Kenneth More as best man, which must have really rubbed salt into Dot's wounds, the ceremony took place at London's Caxton Hall in April 1969—interestingly, Moore gets the year wrong in his memoirs!

The *New of the World*, the doyenne of British scandal rags, lost little time in publishing a feature, headed "The Girl Who Lost The Saint: When Love Turned Sour: Dorothy Squires Talking To Weston Taylor". The ensuing feature claimed that Dot had "sold the intimate story" of her marriage to Roger Moore, which was untrue. Though warned by her lawyer that she would never succeed with such a case against so powerful an organisation, she stuck to her guns, and sued the *News of the World* for "false attribution". The summing-up notes for the defense read:

The words attributed to the plaintiff (Dorothy Squires) were not her words—they were the words

98

of Weston Taylor. The issue was whether the article pretended to be written by Dorothy Squires. The trial judge directed the jury to make up their minds what the impression was to the reader. The jury found that the article did pretend to be written by Dorothy Squires. The Court of Appeal approved the direction by the trial judge and affirmed the decision that the tort had been committed.

Dot was awarded £4,300 in damages and costs of £12,000. Unfortunately this victory over the "establishment" would give her an unhealthy taste for litigation which would almost destroy not just her reputation, but her career.

7: The Great Comeback

"It took me many years to realise that I'd lost Roger for ever. Each woman he ended up with, I always told myself that she was just another flash in the pan, and that once he saw the error of his ways he'd come running back to me. How wrong I was." Dorothy Squires.

This latest drama in Dot's life coincided with her concept album, *The Seasons Of...* released by President. The idea came from her admiration of the traditional French *chanson-réaliste*, which has a beginning, a middle and end—and which eschews the moon-rhymes-with-June banality for lyrics which tear at the emotions. There is little doubting that from this point in her career, Dorothy Squires was no longer just a very good singer—the trials and tribulations of her life, albeit mostly self-inflicted, had transformed her into an exceptional *chanteuse-réaliste*, putting her above the likes of Garland and Streisand, and at times on a par with Edith Piaf.

Like its predecessor with stunning arrangements by Nicky Welsh, the album presents The Dorothy Squires Story so far. The triumphs and tragedies are stripped bare, and no emotion is spared, no matter how raw, how profoundly personal. Like Piaf and Judy, from now on every moment of her life would be shared by those who mattered most—her audiences. The title track, which Dot never performed on the stage, tells of a love affair gone wrong, and is juxtaposed with the seasons: springtime, when she falls in love, summer when she and her lover make plans for a dubious future, autumn when she realises that she has been kidding herself all along, and finally winter when she faces up to reality by concluding of her love for this man, *"No, it never belonged to me."*

There is no question that Dot is *not* referring to Roger Moore, or that the entire theme of the album is focused on him. Indeed, it is the opening of a saga which saw her steadfastly refusing to believe that he had moved on in life. Thus there is profound optimism with Jules Styne's "Just In Time"—the fact that Moore had entered Dot's life when she had been at a low ebb after the acrimonious split from Billy Reid—and this runs into "For Once In My Life", where she declares that the pain, fears and hopelessness of her past are behind her, for she has finally found the love for which she has searched her whole life. Written by Orlando Murden and Ron Miller, the song had been commissioned by Motown Records in 1966, and recorded as a poignant ballad by Barbara McNair, as the composers intended. There had been covers by The Four Tops and Diana Ross, but the most commercially popular version had been Stevie Wonder's recent upbeat rendition, taking it as far from the original as could have been possible. Dot restored it to its former glory.

"A Summer Place" is a direct reference to the love-nests Dot and Moore had shared, first in Bexley then in Hollywood. She follows this with a plea for reassurance by way of Victor Herbert's "Kiss Me Again", before launching the powerful statement of hope that is "Till". Written by Charles Danvers and Pierre Benoit Buisson, this had started out in 1956 as "Priere sans espoir" and provided a big hit on the Continent for the French singer Lucien Rupi. The following year, Carl Sigman had given the song an English lyric and in 1961 Dot's "rival" Shirley Bassey had taken it to Number 14 in the UK charts. Dot's version may perhaps be deemed more definitive in that it reflects what was happening in her life at the time she recorded it. Despite declaring how much she worships the man in her life—defining him as her only reason for being alive—there is still the plea, "Be mine!" at the end.

Side Two of *Seasons of...*opens with "Autumn Leaves", a plaintive of lost love and regret written and composed by

Jacques Prévert and Joseph Kosma as "Les feuilles mortes", and introduced to English-speaking audiences by Edith Piaf and Yves Montand. This leads up the desperation of Leslie Bricusse and Anthony Newley's "Who Can I Turn To?" which Dot performs with an unmistakable sob in her voice as happens with "Point Of No Return", like all the songs on this side of the album, very rarely if ever performed on the stage. By now, she is well aware that she has lost her lover, yet still refuses to admit this. This is followed by the previously mentioned "Where Can I Go?" which sees her hitting notes of unprecedented power as she realises that it really is over between them. Then she sings Charles Trenet's "I Wish You Love", giving the impression that she is no longer bitter and holding grudges against her lover for deserting her—not so of course where Roger Moore was concerned. And the album rounds off with slight optimism as she proclaims, "I Won't Cry Anymore", though we know that she will.

In September 1969, President released the album version of "For Once In My Life" as a single. This was Dot's idea, as a tribute to Judy Garland. She recalled:

> I saw her at the Talk of The Town, the previous December. She was drunk as a lord, and high on whatever she'd just taken. She only managed three songs—one of them was "For Once In My Life"—before the audience started booing and chucking bread rolls at her and shouting for her to get off. People paying top prices for tickets just to make fun of her. She didn't deserve that.

Backed with "Our Garden"—a self-composed song of yearning from the *Say It With Flowers* album—the single lost little time in reaching Number 24 in the hit-parade, and remained in the Top 30 for eleven weeks. In a world where success was all too often measured in revolutions per second, Dorothy Squires had returned!

102

Like Garland, Streisand and Dietrich, Dot had always had a sizeable gay following, but as the new decade dawned she had become *the* quintessential British gay icon. A few years later, she told *OUT*'s Mike Dow of how she had once been actively involved with a gay Christian group in America:

> I'm very grateful for whatever draws gay people into my concerts and for the dedication and encouragement in their letters. I once went to a gay church service in California and it absolutely opened my eyes. Before, I used to feel sympathy, but I don't any more. We're all in the same category. It makes no difference. It's a love and a tremendous love. I was very sad when a couple of years later that church burnt down....Gays have meant a great deal to me. I can't define it, and I don't suppose they could.

To which Dow responded, referring to the term which had sprung up in the wake of *The Wizard of Oz* and the Judy Garland character's acceptance of men who were different—i.e., The Scarecrow, The Tin Man and The Cowardly Lion—"How true. But I think we should all be proud to be a Friend of Dorothy."

In February 1970, President released a follow-up single, "Till"—not the album version, which Dot said would rip off the fans who already had this, but a new arrangement by Nicky Welsh. With "The Seasons Of" on the flip-side this also reached Number 24 in the hit-parade, and remained in the charts for eleven weeks. Her biggest hit, however, was her stunning, from the heart rendition of "My Way", which had a new version of "With All My Heart" on the flipside.

"My Way" had started out as "Comme d'habitude" (As Usual) in 1967, composed by Claude Francois and Jacques Rivaux for the French singer Hervé Vilard, and with lyrics by Gilles Thibault. Francois had also recorded it, but in France the most successful version was by Michel Sardou. Paul Anka had acquired translation rights the following year, with the proviso being that the original authors retain equal share of the royalties. Anka frequently boasted that *he* had written the song for a friend—Frank Sinatra, who had a massive hit with it—but it was essentially Francois' creation. The French lyrics, about a man getting up on a morning and going about his daily business, "as usual", have nothing in common with Anka's, though his lyrics—about someone who has "reached the final curtain" and is now reflecting on their life with but few regrets—are more appropriate to some of those who recorded the song, most especially Sinatra and Dorothy Squires, the only female singer who charted with a song said to have been covered more than any other with the exception of Lennon and McCartney's "Yesterday". Dot's version shot into the UK charts and though it only peaked at Number 25 in August 1970—whilst Sinatra's had reached the top spot—it remained in the Top 30 for over six months and was immediately adopted by her as her signature tune, opening and closing every show. What made its success even more astonishing is that it received virtually no airplay, save on independent radio stations, and even when in the charts Dot was not invited to perform it on television. Therefore she was pushed into seriously taking stock of her life, as she explained:

> My husband had left me for a younger model. None of the major theatres wanted to hire me, and I was hardly ever on the television or radio, I'm convinced because of the nasty things people were saying about me behind my back, when *I* was the one being shat on, though of course I did play Roger at his own game. So I said to myself, "If the theatre managers don't want me, the fans certainly do, and if the theatre managers don't want to hire me for their theatres, then I'll hire the theatres myself!

Of the song "My Way" she told Sally Clyde:

> Oh, please God! I'll always bite off more than I can chew. It means each day I reach for something higher, aim at something bigger. And it works. People advise you right, left and centre...but in the end you always do it your way!

Any other spurned singer might have started out by hiring one of the smaller theatres out in the sticks. In her memoirs, Dot recalls calling Ted Gollop of Moss Empires, towards the end of September, to ask how much it would to hire the very pinnacle of British entertainment—the London Palladium. He called her back a few days later. The venture would set her back a cool £5,000. For now, she kept the news to herself because she had "other urgent fish to fry" as she flew out to Gibraltar to participate in what was to be a very important event in the island's turbulent history and ongoing row over sovereignty.

In 1966, Spain had closed the border with Gibraltar, and the next year the Gibraltar International Song Festival had been launched. One of the jury members was Brian Willey—a producer with the BBC who had worked on the television show, *On the Scene*. A massive Squires fan, Willey told the story of how, when billeted at RAF Debden after World War II, the recruits had adopted her "Unchangeable You", written by Billy Reid, as their anthem. By 1969, Willey and another jury member, Ronnie Bridges, had composed "The Gibraltar Anthem" and submitted it for entry into the contest, using pseudonyms. It had been rejected when the organisers had learned their identities, but a compromise offered—providing they could find a singer who would bring "guts" to the piece, it would be permitted as "interval entertainment" for the 1970 contest. Willey had worked with Dot and they were friends. He asked her to perform the song, and she accepted without hesitation. The event, on 14 November, saw her appearing in her most unconventional venue ever—St Michael's Cave, a 500-seater auditorium halfway up the Rock, filled with stalactites and stalagmites but offering perfect acoustics—and such was her reception that she reprised the song three times! Afterwards, she signed all 1,000 numbered copies of the limited edition sheet music—the first of which was later presented to Queen Elizabeth II.

On 23 November Dot gave a press-statement at the Palladium: her show would take place on 6 December, and would be recorded and released—"warts and all"—on a double album. She chose this date because of its personal significance: five years since her Llanelli comeback shows, fourteen years since the premiere of *Stars In Your Eyes* and thirty-five years since she had cut her first record. Within three hours of the box-office opening, all 2,300 tickets had been sold. Such was the demand, she could have filled the venue for an entire week. Yet no sooner had she signed the contract than she began having doubts, as she observes in the album's sleeve-notes:

> I saw the headlines in the press, "Dorothy Squires Hires The London Palladium". Then it hit me what I had done. Had I bitten off more than I could chew? Because if I had failed in this venture, I could never work on a stage again. But I was strangely calm. I was not bothered about the money, but I would suddenly shiver thinking of the consequences if all I had planned would blow up in my face. The chance I took was on you, the public. The faith I had was in you, the public. Your letters told me what I wanted to know, and you didn't let me down. And for the first time in my life I felt my prayers had reached God's ears.

She told me, "Would you believe that I'd hired the Grand Theatre in Wolverhampton? Then I said to myself when I was driving down Oxford Street, "Well, that *may* be such a wonderful place. But why not go for make or break and hire the Palladium and *really* give my oppressors something to talk about?"

Though her friends knew exactly who she was referring to, Dot did not reveal the names of her "oppressors" at the time. Seven years later, in an interview for Harlech Television during a return to Llanelli, she did not hold back:

> We have a tremendous monopoly in the business. We have one of the most devastating monopolies in show business. It's frightening. I've worked in practically every country in the world and I've *never* known a monopoly. And, incidentally, I have taken the monopoly very much to task. They can't hurt me any more. They need *me*, now. I don't suppose I'll ever be televised by these people. I'm talking about the establishment. In other words Lord Delfont, Lord Grade and Leslie Grade.

Asked why she believed that her face did not fit, she replied:

> How does one know? You see, if you scare them they say how *dare* you be a success and hire the Palladium and pack it, and prove them wrong? I've done nothing to them. I was knocking my head against a brick wall...

Her interviewer asked how hard she thought it was for the new generation of entertainers to get onto the show business ladder. Dot defended them so virulently, one can see her fighting not to let rip with those infamous Squires expletives:

> I've had talent on bills with me, and it's frightening that they'll never see the light of day...because if their face doesn't fit, they'll *never* become stars.

107

Later she told *Reveille's* Margaret Pride, "Some came to laugh and leer, some because they thought I must be a freak."

One of the detractors who had never liked Dot was the feisty *Daily Mail* columnist, Lynda Lee-Potter. Under the heading, "Don't Do It, Dot! You Can't Buy Success!" she scathed:

> She is laying herself open to defeat, derision and a public humiliation of such magnitude she'll never get over it. Years ago audiences queued for hours to see her. She didn't have to hire a theatre and *give away* tickets.

Intimating that Lee-Potter was "sick in the head", Dot had a huge Get Well Soon card delivered to her office, upon which she had written:

> For once I fully agree with you. No one can buy success. If they could, the millionaires would buy the lot, and keep it for themselves and their children—and *their* children. I am paying for the chance to prove what I can do, having been in the charts three times in the last eighteen months. Dear Linda, *you'll* have to pay black market prices to get in because my comeback sold out in a day.

For what is regarded by many as the greatest performance of her career Dot had engaged the cream of British musicianship—at a cost of £3,000 for that one evening. Nicky Welsh—she refused to even consider anyone else—conducted the Charlie Katz Orchestra. Kenny Brown—at his best *almost* as good as Russ Conway—would remain her personal accompanist for the rest of her career. Likewise saxophonist Johnnie Gray (1920-2014), who had started out with the Ted Heath Orchestra in 1945 and in a varied career had recorded with

Dusty Springfield, Nat King Cole, Matt Monro, and with the Beatles on their *Sgt Pepper's Lonely Hearts Club Band* album. To describe Johnnie as a colourful character may be an understatement. There was the drummer, Mac Swann, and finally the Tony Mansell Choir. Setting another precedent, Dot's white, feather-trimmed gown was designed by Douglas Darnell (1933-2012), the former window-dresser for C & A's Oxford Street store who had gone on to clad such luminaries as Marlene Dietrich, Shirley Bassey, Zsa Zsa Gabor, Dot's friend, Diana Dors, who recommended him to her—and some of Danny La Rue's gowns which he wore when impersonating her!

It was a very apprehensive Dorothy Squires who walked on to the stage of the Palladium that night. She was introduced by the actor Simon Oates, currently appearing in television's *Doomwatch* series. Ironically, two years later he would be in the running to play James Bond in *Live And Let Die*, a part which eventually went to...Roger Moore. As had happened in Llanelli, Dot sang the autobiographical banter between segments and embellished some of the songs themselves with her own words, as she does in her opening number, "Back In Your Own Back Yard", which runs into Ray Stevens' recent hit, "Everything Is Beautiful". For now there would be no complaints from their composers—most of them were content to have her performing their work—though as will be seen there would be problems later on when she began using them as props for her brushes with the law. She then launched into Bobby Worth's "Do I Worry?" which she had recorded back in 1950. With Dot pulling out all the stoppers, this was clearly aimed at Roger Moore. Next up was her "River Medley", and after bringing the house down with "For Once In My Life" comes her "Autograph Book" sequence—a regular feature in her recitals from now on.

Anyone seeing Dot for the first time and unaware of what was happening would fall for the ruse of her secretary, Hilda Brown (and occasionally Doris Gaard, who ran her fan club) rushing up to the stage with an autograph book, claiming that she was in a hurry and had a bus to catch—and Dot saying that if she waited until the end of the show she would sign the book, and pay for the "fan" to go home in a taxi, only to be told that she lived at the other end of the country. In this first one, she pays homage to Barbra Streisand with "Why Did I Choose You", Piaf with "If You Love Me, Really Love Me", Judy Garland with "The Man That Got Away"—another reference of course to Roger Moore—and finally to herself, by way of Frank Sinatra, with "My Way". If Dot had initially worried about falling flat on her face, the hysterical applause brought about by this and "Till", her own autograph song, was more than sufficient to convince her that she had made the right move in hiring the Palladium for her comeback.

After her "Wonderful" memory, Dot pleaded "Don't Take Your Love From Me", introduced by Mildred Bailey in 1940, but until now largely forgotten—not that there was any chance of this happening, as proved by the subsequent five-minute standing ovation. After "It's The Talk of the Town" came her own "It Can't Be Done", composed just days earlier especially for this show, and "The Gibraltar Anthem". After "Didn't We" and "Say It With Flowers", Dot went into the story medley she had first performed in Llanelli, telling the story of her association with Billy Reid which might have been better had this been placed earlier on in her recital, or even eschewed altogether for a medley of Reid songs as would happen in the future. And finally, she proclaimed her triumph in the face of adversity with her own "I Can Live Again", and rounded off the proceedings with "I've Gotta Be Me"—an absolute triumph!

The press plaudits were legion for a recital which in effect was no less important than Piaf's famous December 1960 Paris Olympia premiere and Judy's equally legendary one at Carnegie Hall the following April. James Green, one of Dot's foremost champions, observed in the *London Evening News*:

110

Garland and Edith Piaf may have vanished but the breed survives through the tiny body and booming, emotive voice of Dorothy Squires. Like the other two, she gives an appearance of defenceless frailty which disguises a mercurial temperament, cast-iron will and battler's constitution.

Douglas Marlborough wrote in the *Daily Sketch*:

> There were fantastic scenes outside the Palladium before the three-hour show started. A policeman said, "Crikey, don't tell me the Beatles are back!"...Dorothy Squires proved to the world last night that she is still a star. After receiving the biggest reception at the Palladium for years, she said almost in a whisper, "Now I can die happy!"

The next morning, a jubilant Dot told Robert Peart of the *Evening News*, "It's been a smack in the eye for those who said I was foolish to try. At last I seem to have broken the monopoly which has kept me away from the public eye for so long. My reception last night has shown the critics. This is the most wonderful moment of my life."

For Dot the success of *Palladium 70* opened those doors which had previously been slammed in her face. But she was a woman who bore grudges, in most cases rightly so, and did not take to being pandered to. She told me:

> I accepted a season at the Talk of Town because that bastard Robert Nesbitt wasn't involved this time. As for those provincial theatre managers who previously said they wouldn't have me in their theatres for all the tea in China, they were not so politely told where to shove their offers.

Of her premiere the *London Evening News*' James Green took a cynical swipe at the "establishment", on her behalf:

I reckon ex-champ Dave Charnley was bang on target when he said of Dorothy Squires, "Thank God I never met you in the ring!" As a performer, a knock-out specialist, she has a better constitution than the British Commonwealth....She says to heck with the past. She loves the whole world. Loves the police, the BBC, the record pluggers, and wants the whole world to love her. Her final plea is "Don't Take Your Love From Me"....She makes her own rules and goes her own way and if you change her, then you wouldn't have the original artist who sang, cooed and belted her way out of obscurity.

Dot also triumphed in a season at the Latin Quarter, the plush if not then "iffy" cabaret on London's Wardour Street, smack in the heart of the gay village.

"Each time I came out on stage, I looked around the tables next to the stage to see if anybody looked like they were with the bloody Mafia," Dot recalled. "Some very shifty characters used to go there, I can tell you. Cut-throats and gangsters!"

The Latin Quarter was a haunt much favoured by East End gangsters, such as those members of the Kray and Charlie Richardson gangs who were not in jail. The previous year, the *Carry On* actress Barbara Windsor's brother-in-law, David Knight, had been stabbed to death here by the doorman, Alfredo "Eyetie Tony" Zomparelli, a big Squires fan who often dropped into her dressing-room, though by the time I became part of her entourage he was behind bars. Zomparelli was released just in time to catch one of her shows, and what surprised me was that the softly-spoken, avuncular man that I met and shook hands with after his release was a dangerous thug. In September 1974, he was gunned down whilst playing the pinball machine in the arcade he owned nearby. Knight and his friend Nicky Gerard, another Squires fan, were arrested in connection with the killing but not convicted, though Knight later confessed in his memoirs that he had given orders to Gerard to have Zomparelli taken out. Gerard himself was gunned down in a Soho street in 1982.

"This was one of the most thrilling and exciting first nights I have been to," Robert Gaddes enthused in *What's On In London*. "No wonder Dorothy Squires was given a standing ovation—something I've *never* seen before at the Latin Quarter."

Neil Stevens observed in the *Evening Mail*:

A tornado swept into Wardour Street last night, whirling all in its wake. None other than Dorothy Squires, back where she belonged. Swinging higher than any kite she nevertheless came down bang on the right note, sizzling her way through a score of favourites with the might of a bulldozer. Miss Squires at first stroked a number as though it was a sweet, gentle dog. Then she proceeded to wring its neck in the nicest melodic way....Without doubt she is a terrific entertainer. She belts 'em loud all right, and I trust the management have all the glass on the premises fully insured.

The Palladium comeback, 6 December 1970

8: The Payola Scandal

"When the News of the World published 'When Love Turned Sour', that was the beginning of the end for me because of the vendetta I was subjected to after that. And I hold Rupert Murdoch entirely responsible for it." Dorothy Squires.

In her memoirs, Dot wrote that walking on stage every night and hearing the applause and chants of "We love you, Dot!" had finally convinced her that her love for Roger Moore was over. She had been searching, she said, for a reason why her marriage and Moore's love for her had ended so abruptly, and was now convinced that God had nurtured other plans for her back then and that only now was she reaping their rewards.

Over the next year, Dot accepted offers to sing in theatres which had *not* rejected her in the past and, in rival theatres in towns and cities where she had been made to feel unwelcome, she still booked them herself. On 27 August 1971, I saw Dot for the first time at the Sheffield Fiesta. My mother had died in June, and to cheer me up my father in a rare act of kindness bought tickets for the show. I distinctly remember a young man rushing up to the front of the stage after Dot had sung "My Way" to present her with a spray of flowers. Dot read out the writing on the card, and had the audience in hysterics. It was the man's wedding anniversary, and he had given the flowers meant for his wife to Dot!

Yet despite the dozens of sell-out concerts all over Britain since her Palladium comeback, despite the adulation and chart successes, 1971 kicked off with an ordeal which would see Dot targeted by spurned peers from the entertainment world for three more years, for no other reason than she had given them a taste of their own medicine—in proving that she could manage without them, if need be. Relentlessly she was dragged into the so-called "Payola Scandal". In the eyes of these hypocrites, *because* Dot had "done things her way", it figured that her three singles could only have got into the charts because *she* had forked out bribes to guarantee them airplay, at a time when radio stations had been giving her the cold shoulder. This was of course untrue.

Her ordeal began on 21 February 1971 when the *News of the World* ran the banner headline, "Scandal at the BBC". The accompanying feature declared that undercover reporters had recently conducted "a massive investigation", and assembled "an astonishing story of what goes on among producers, DJs, and the fixers from the pop record business who batten on them." The paper's "dossier of details" was revealed:

> PAYOLA: cash payments to obtain plugs for records.
> *The use of call-girls to entertain well-known BBC personalities.
> *Deceit by producers and disc-jockeys who use the BBC to push records in which they have a personal financial interest.
> *Disguised inducements: all expenses paid holidays and trips abroad.
> *Rigging of the "Top 20 Record Charts which computerisation is supposed to have made foolproof.
> *Girl "record pluggers" working on a "bed-for-plug basis".

The editorial continued:

> Clandestine deals with BBC employees over cash payments, lavish favours and the provision of sex parties are commonplace. Exactly how many record pluggers work on a "bed-in-return-for-plugs"

basis is anybody's guess, but this form of sexual payola is certainly commonplace.

The feature concluded, claiming that this had been confirmed by a top record company executive:

Direct payments to obtain plugs for records were rife among certain producers and disc-jockeys.

Dot had always suspected that the record charts might have been fixed—they were not—and was therefore "hell-bent" on having her say, whether this got her into hot water or not. She called the editors of every major British newspaper, none of whom wanted to or even dared comment on an issue which involved an ongoing *News of the World* investigation, and which allegedly was employing undercover journalists posing as tea ladies, office boys and cleaners and, according to Dot later on, even sex-workers to infiltrate record companies and the BBC, and report back with any little snippet they could find as had happened in America during the *Confidential* magazine scandal. With incredible nerve, she called Sir Charles Curran, the director general of the BBC, who understandably wanted nothing to do with her. When all else failed, she contacted the pirate radio stations—few of which played her style of music. Then she remembered a disc-jockey fan called Ed Moreno (Norman Cole, 1933-80), who had played her records on Radio Caroline when joining the station in 1964. I distinctly remember him attending some of her concerts during the early Seventies—a robust-looking but very poorly man who suffered from severe diabetes, who qualified as a doctor after leaving broadcasting and, unable to cope with his illness any longer, tragically took his own life.

Years later, Dot told *OUT*'s Mike Dow what she would never have dared confess to anyone at the time the Payola investigation was in full-swing:

117

I once went to Holland and faced arrest to try and get my records played on Radio Caroline. I risked a six months' sentence, if any of us were found supporting the independent commercial ships. But it was the worst storm that ever raged, and maybe it was a Godsend because I would have faced the sentence if I knew what was being planned for me.

This story was not wholly true. On 27 February 1971, six days after the *News of the World* headline, Ed Moreno called Dot from Scheveningen, in the Netherlands. He was about to give his first broadcast not for Radio Caroline, but for RNI (Radio Northsea International) from the *Mebo II*, moored off the Dutch coast, and having heard of her plight invited her on to his show for an in-depth interview. By the time she arrived in Scheveningen there *was* a storm, but the mercurial Moreno had already given notice to leave RNI, after making just one broadcast, following a bust-up with the bosses. As Dot's interview had been advertised and as he was such a fan, he agreed to interview her on dry land. Their talk, billed as a live broadcast was recorded on 7 March and some of Dot's more colourful comments removed. It went out on RNI the following evening.

It is an eye-opener in which Dot did herself few favours. It begins with Moreno telling his listeners that the last time he and Dot met, they had "one hell of an argument".

"It was backstage, at one my shows," she told me. "He said that I didn't have *that* many wrinkles, considering how old I was. Then he laughed it off as a joke, and I told him to bugger off and never cross my path again."

For ten very tense minutes, scarcely pausing for breath and getting increasingly irate, Dot rattles off her grievances against the compilers of the record charts:

We've got to do something, Ed. There are three or four different charts, and basically it all comes back to the one thing. These charts are bent.

She then goes on to explain that, though "Till" had sold 40,000 copies in three weeks, it had only reached Number 44 in the charts whilst she had it on good authority that the record two places below her, at Number 46, had sold only 2,000 copies. Then she starts to dig herself into very deep hole so far as the Payola scandal is concerned, bearing in mind that at that very moment, the BBC were being scrutinised by the *News of the World*:

> I don't know whether you know it, but the BBC pay £10,000 a year for these charts to be compiled, and it's public money. And on top of that *every* record company contribute, I think [contribute] something like £750 a year.

Moreno next asks her if she knows of any other artiste who is in the same position as herself, selling lots of records, but not moving up the charts—she cites Dusty Springfield, who she says she admires. On and on she rants, not finishing one sentence before she starts another, often not making much sense at all until Moreno decides to bring the interview to an uncomfortable close:

> I'm going to do something which is unprecedented in radio. I'm going to give you half a minute to say *whatever* you like to the public or to the people who compile the charts. The air time's yours.

Earlier in the interview, Dot had explained how she had called the managing editor of the *New Musical Express*, Britain's top-selling weekly music publication:

> I said, "How do you compile your charts?" and he said, "That's our business." I said, "No, it's my business. This is *public* business!"

And, now that Moreno had given her the chance to explain

her predicament, and with no one at hand to censor her, she let rip:

> Right! Now, I asked the editor of the NME...I made a survey of "Once In My Life", I phoned the editor, he refused to give me information, but unfortunately for him the managing editor [she means managing director] had given me that information when I had "Say It With Flowers". Now I know how the charts are compiled. They're done by their accountants. Now I ask you, Ed. Need I say any more? They do it themselves!

The interview did not end here, though. Now that Dot was into her stride, so to speak, she became relentless with her name-dropping and expletives. This meant that the last five minutes of the interview could not be broadcast at all, much to the relief of the bosses at RNI who shuddered to think what might have happened had this been broadcast live! But she had made her point—and dug herself into the hole from which she *would* safely emerge, but which nevertheless would set her on the very stony pathway to being eventually declared a "vexatious litigant".

In the *News of the World*'s 21 March edition, more revelations were published and the focus was on *Top of the Pops*, where the suggestion was made that girls appearing in the audience were being put in "moral danger". The piece concluded, "Nowhere in our inquiries did we discover such appalling disregard for the well-being of pop-crazy youngsters."

On 4 April, the paper announced that the Payola allegations could be grouped under four main headings:

> 1: Allegations that producers and disc jockeys had received payment in cash or in kind, including sexual favours, in return for the playing of records on BBC programmes.

2: Allegations that producers and disc jockeys had used their position at the BBC to promote records in which they themselves had some financial interest.

3: Allegations concerning the programme *Top of the Pops*.

4: Allegations that the Top 20 record charts had been rigged.

In its series of "exclusives", the *News of the World* expanded on some of the alleged "rewards" being doled out to certain BBC executives, producers and disc jockeys—at sex-parties which had taken place in the singer Janie Jones apartment in Kensington's Campden Hill Road. There were reports of two-way mirrors so that those not involved in the action could watch discreetly, whilst prostitutes and rent boys were provided at West End hotels for "peers of the realm, diplomats, and Arab kings and princes".

An independent enquiry was launched by Brian Neill QC. For years his report was not made public, and only then with the names of those still alive blanked out. After his death in 2005, the disc jockey Tommy Vance was named as "King of the Orgies" whilst Jimmy Savile was questioned by the police and it is believed by Neill personally. He refused to cooperate in the enquiry—not only this, it emerged that he had made fun of the on-duty solicitor for even suggesting that he might have behaved "inappropriately". Dot recalled:

> It was all hushed up. Everyone in authority at the BBC was well aware that Jimmy Savile was a pervert who preyed on young women—in particular that poor girl who killed herself, but he was so big that no one dared expose him. Neither was he the only one. So they went for Janie Jones, Jack Dabbs and myself.

121

"That poor girl" was Clair McAlpine, a 15-year-old dancer on *Top of the Pops* who told the police that she had been sexually abused by DJs, and committed suicide three months after the story broke. It was later alleged that Claire had detailed in the diary what Savile and others had done to her. Under the headline, "Scotland Yarders Bust 9 In BBC Payola Scandal", the broadcaster Paul Gambaccini and his colleague Andrew Bailey sarcastically revealed in a syndicated feature:

> Dorothy Squires, a middle-aged cabaret singer known for her temper tantrums, became suspicious the morning of May 17th. A car had been parked outside her house since dawn. She telephoned police to have them check it out; shortly afterward, the two men in the car were joined by three others. Together they went to the singer's door, and presented themselves as detectives carrying a warrant for her arrest in connection with allegations that BBC producers had been bribed to give certain records airplay. Before taking her away the detectives waited until Ms. Squires, the former wife of actor Roger Moore, ate breakfast and donned a matching mink coat and hat.

Amongst the hundred or so reported to have been questioned or arrested at around the same time (in the press and the subsequent Neill Report) were record promoter Roger Bolton, producer Clive Crawley, accused of offering cash to BBC agents, and theatrical agent Leonard Tucker, accused of conspiring to rig record charts. All three members of the New World pop group (John Kane, Mel Noonan, John Lee) were accused of contravening the Forgery Act, in which they had rigged the result on ITV's *Opportunity Knocks* by sending in postcards and voting for themselves to win. Ed Kassner, the head of President Records, faced a more serious charge, of paying to have records played on BBC television's *Disco 2 and* of helping Janie Jones to procure the services of prostitutes "to such agents of the BBC as may be induced to accept them as an inducement or reward." Also arrested was a disc jockey identified only as "Mr. T." who later confessed to having been involved in a three-men, three-women sex orgy at Jones' home in November, despite having his leg in plaster at the time—though he stressed that he had not paid for the privilege of having so much fun.

Jones and her "accomplice" Eric Gilbert were charged with "prostitution, demanding money with menaces, intimidating witnesses, obtaining money by deception and lying to obtain a divorce." Jones' ex-husband, John Christian Dee, was charged with intimidation. Dot and Jack Dabbs, who produced the BBC's Sunday lunchtime programme *Family Favourites* were summoned to court on 15 June 1973 on a charge of hit-parade fixing, the accusation being that Dabbs had accepted from Dot all-expenses paid trips to Malta and other destinations in exchange for playing her three President singles on the radio. Jones wrote in her memoirs:

> At Bow Street I was put in a cell with Dorothy. It was a horrific and disgusting experience. There was excrement all over the floor and walls. To make matters worse, Dorothy suffered from claustrophobia. She's never been able to ride in a lift at the record company offices, so she started banging on the door with a shoe. "Let us out," she shrieked. "We're stars, we're not criminals, you bastards!" She was effing and blinding like mad. "You silly old bag," the coppers shouted back. "You're not stars in here, you're prisoners."…They were definitely getting their jollies out of it all, seeing Dorothy under pressure and cracking jokes about her age. So I sat calmly in the cell and tried to comfort Dorothy, confident that I'd soon be home

for a cup of tea. Unfortunately, I wouldn't see my kettle for a very long time.

The week before the hearing, Dot had returned to Wales to tape a guest-slot on BBC Wales' Welsh language variety show, *Ryan & Ronnie*. This was now scrapped, and when Dot wrote to the corporation's chairman, Sir Michael Swann, asking why, she received a snooty response:

> The placing of any programme is a matter wholly within the discretion of the BBC, and it has been decided not to place the Dorothy Squires slot in the *Ryan & Ronnie Show* for the time being.

"Bastards, the lot of them," was Dot's response. "Talk about kicking someone when they're down. Even when I've been found innocent, they're still treating me like a criminal!"

Dot was forthright when recounting her brushes with the law to *OUT*'s Mike Dow:

> I've been in stinking cells with stinking mattresses and walls covered with night secretions. I've had water thrown over me and shared cells with whores, dope addicts, and once even a murderess.

She revealed in her memoirs that until reading about Janie Jones in the *News of the World*, she had never heard of her, let alone visited her house, and that the first time they *had* met was in the police cell. She recalls how people began asking her if she had enjoyed the orgies at Jones' house, that the situation had become *so* distressing that she contemplated suicide. She writes that because of the scandal she, who had packed theatres to the rafters, had found herself playing to half-capacity audiences. I cannot vouch for Dot's state of mind, how she felt when the curtain came down and she returned home or to her hotel. She got tearful sometimes, which was only to be expected—but I never attended a Squires concert at the time that was *not* a sold-out event. She told me:

> The tabloid journalists were the worst. I don't have to tell you which papers they were working for. One of them asked me if I'd paid to have my records plugged or whether I'd got on my back and paid them in kind. Doris [Gaard], bless her, small as she was held me back from kicking the bastard in the balls, otherwise I'd have spent another night in a cell and been up on an assault charge."

The next day the headline in the *Daily Express* proclaimed, "Payola Swoop After Plugging Probe", whilst the *Sun* stuck with their customary titillation approach and announced, "Bribes, Threats, Conspiracy, Sex". Dot had told reporters, "I'm innocent. I passed out three times while the police questioned me. Scotland Yard are wasting public money and public time."

At the Old Bailey trial in November 1974, Jones would be found guilty and sentenced to three years in Holloway. Dot and Jack Dabbs were not asked to take the stand, and all charges against them were dropped as there was no evidence that bribery had taken place—Dabbs provided the court with written proof that he had paid for the Malta and Gibraltar trips himself. Outside the court, Dot was mobbed by fans and gave a statement to the press:

> I deeply regret that I never had the chance to address the court. It would have been the performance of my life. It would have been the simple truth, from the heart. No one who knows me could ever believe that I would do anything so corrupt—or that I would be so stupid and wicked, to

imperil the position of Jack Dabbs who has worked for the BBC for thirty years. I have never done anything underhand in my life.

Asked how she was going to celebrate, now that she had been cleared, whilst hugging one of her fans, Dot excitedly told the *Daily Mirror*'s George Glenton:

> I am going immediately to hire the Palladium. If I can't get the Palladium, then I will get the Royal Festival Hall. And if I can't get the Royal Festival Hall, I'll hire a hall where fans can see me in London. This has nearly put me in the grave. I have never been guilty of the things they said about me. It has been four [sic] years of humiliation.

Dabbs (according to Dot) reeled off an anonymous letter to Trevor Kempson and Clive Cooke, the *News of the World* journalists who had broken the Payola story, informing them that he would not like to be "in their shoes for all the tea in China". This exact phrase is included in an uncensored entry dated 8 March 1971 in the *Neill Report* disclosure documents (needleblog.wordpress.com) in which the sender predicts that "within six months you will be six feet under or behind the bars of Wormwood Scrubs". They also reveal the names of several men—disc-jockeys, pop stars and politicians—guilty of "accepting sex as payola". With the exception of Tommy Vance (deceased by the time the document was published), these were blanked out. For her part, Dot issued the News of the World with a High Court writ, not just against the newspaper but against Trevor Kempson and Clive Cooke. Ten years down the line, she was still fuming:

> They were tinkering around with the wrong person. I'd done nothing wrong. My records were selling because my fans wanted to buy them, *not* because

I paid to have them played on the radio. And those journalists weren't practicing what they preached. One was into prostitutes, and the other one—well, we won't go into that. And as for that man who owned the *News of the World...*

I will not repeat what Dot said about Cooke and Rupert Murdoch. As for Kempson, this self-proclaimed "moral family man" succumbed to AIDS—acquired it is thought from a prostitute he consorted with at one of the very sex parties he was investigating.

The case left an aftertaste of bitterness. Henceforth Dot would take out writs against anyone she believed was "out to get her", and rarely with successful results, as shall be seen. She was convinced that the police had her "marked as a target", never missing an opportunity to victimise her—such as the occasion she was stopped on suspicion of driving under the influence of alcohol, and asked to take to breathalyser. She told *Reveille*'s Margaret Pride:

> Breathalyser! I was taking pills at the time and wasn't ALLOWED to drink. What made me so angry was the way the police stopped my car, opened the door, and said, 'You are going to blow into this little bag.' I refused because of their attitude. So I was carted off to the clink and a policewoman said, "Come on, Flossie—get your arms up." "Don't call *me* Flossie," I said to her.

Dot still refused to take the test, allegedly hit a policeman, and was hauled before a judge, who cleared her of the charge, but not without denouncing her behaviour as "obstreperous".

"That's me," she chuckled. "I bet the old bugger couldn't even spell it!"

Dot, pictured during the Dutch radio broadcast.

Cleared of involvement in the BBC Payola Scandal, a jubilant Dot is congratulated outside the court by a fan.

"Me, with all the slap washed off, cooling off after by biggest ordeal!"

9: Solitude's My Home

"It always baffled me why Dot had other people on the bill with her. At every show I played at, nobody was remotely interested in these mostly third-rate so-called entertainers and comedians. All they wanted was Dot, Dot, Dot!" Johnnie Gray, saxophonist.

On 5 December 1971, a year to the day almost since her greatest triumph, with the same musicians and orchestra leader, Dot hired the Palladium for a concert which sold out in less than an hour. As before the performance was recorded, and the album proved a best-seller. Introduced by Pete Murray, she opened with James Last's "Happy Heart", changing the words to suit the way she claimed she felt, though privately, with all that was going on, she was anything but happy. Her "new" songs included "Where Do I Begin?" from *Love Story*, "Bewitched", and her own "When There's Love In Your Heart". It was not long before she was expressing her disappointment over losing the great love of her life with "There Goes My Heart" and "If He Walked Into My Life" from *Mame*, whilst there was an optimistic shrug of the shoulders with Paul Anka's "Life Goes On". There was a new autograph book sequence: Louis Armstrong's "What a Wonderful World", Shirley Bassey's "As Long As He Needs Me", Danny La Rue's "On Mother Kelly's Doorstep" and her own "Mother's Day". The highlight of the recital was hers and Ernie Dunstall's 15-minute *Irony of War* medley. This included Pete Seeger's "Where Have All the Flowers Gone", Don Black's thought-provoking "When The World Is Ready" from *The Long Duel*; "The Battle Hymn Of The Republic"; music-hall songs "It's A Long Way To Tipperary", "Goodbye Dolly Gray" and "Pack Up Your Troubles In Your Old Kit Bag" —and "Maman".

The latter, which President put out as a single—backed with Dot's and Mark Eden's "Don't Ask Me Why"—was one of the most moving songs she ever sang. It came from the musical, *Mata Hari*. With lyrics by Edward Thomas and music by Martin Charnin, it opened in Washington in 1967, produced and directed by Vincente Minnelli. The story centres around the celebrated dancer's love affair with a French intelligence officer, and parallels that of a soldier fighting in the trenches. It is he who performs the song, recalling in a letter to his mother his fear of going into battle, how he shook, wondering if when the time came he would have courage to face the foe, and then telling her what happened when he did:

> *He was young, maman, he was small,*
> *Then he lunged, maman, and I spun,*
> *Face to face, maman, gun to gun,*
> *Just a boy, maman, not yet a man,*
> *Can I kill, maman? Yes, I can…*

Dot wanted to perform the song—at eight minutes, the longest she ever sang—when she topped the bill on ATV's *Saturday Variety* on 22 January 1972, but as this was way too long, she opted three numbers of her choice, thrilling the audience and topping that week's television ratings with "Happy Heart", "For Once In My Life" and "My Way".

On 1 March, Dot was amongst the guests, along with the cast of the comedy series *Nearest and Dearest*, who took part in Hylda Baker's *This Is Your Life*. Though she had no problem being a participant she did make a point of telling Eamonn Andrews that, if he ever sprang his famous red book on her, she would "do a Danny Blanchflower". In 1961, the Tottenham Hotspur midfielder had stormed away from Andrews, telling him, "I consider this programme to be an invasion of privacy."

On 16 April 1972 Dot performed "Maman" on ITV's *The Golden Shot*, reducing the host Norman Vaughan to tears. It was its reception—a three minute ovation on live television which resulted in the next programme running late—which prompted her to make her biggest gamble so far, performing her *Irony of War* medley at New York's Carnegie Hall!

"It was an act of extreme insanity, but it was something I felt I had to do," she said. "For years, Carnegie Hall had been known for its classical concerts, but Piaf and Judy Garland had changed all that. So I got my pal Richard Armitage to arrange everything."

Richard Armitage (1926-86) was the son of songwriter and music publisher Noel Gay. Dot had met him by way of Russ Conway, who he managed for a time. His later celebrity clients would include John Cleese, Stephen Fry, and French singer Claude Francois, who had given the world "My Way". At a cost of £25,000—on top of which it would cost £5,000 to take her orchestra with her—Dot hired the venue for 22 October 1972, and for an undisclosed fee thought to have been only slightly less hired the Los Angeles Music Center. No sooner had the cash been handed over than the managers of both venues told Richard Armitage that she would not be permitted to do her *Irony of War* medley because the Vietnam War was in full-swing. Dot recalled:

> When Piaf did Carnegie Hall, she was told not do some of her songs about prostitutes and suicide and war, but sang them just the same. So when I got there and nothing could be done about it I told the manager, "I don't tell you how to do your job, so don't tell me how to do mine boyo. And in any case,

132

who's paying for this gaff?" Then he said, "Aha, you're Welsh. Do you know Shirley Bassey and Tom Jones?" The daft bugger!

She had told Jim Greensmith of the *Sheffield Star*.

> There are only two ways of going down big in America. One is with a hit record, the other is to make an impact straight away. It's no good going there looking for work. So Carnegie Hall is really a glorified audition. If it pays off, what you could earn could be astronomical.

Doris Gaard chartered a plane for 172 privileged members of Dot's fan club to fly out to New York and offer support, and to respond to her between-numbers patter about the ups and downs of her private life which almost certainly would have been lost on an all-American audience. One such was the *London Evening News'* James Green, who recalled how she was more nervous than usual until receiving her first standing ovation—after her second song. Also, unlike most of her British shows, as with Judy and Piaf she was the only artiste on the bill, performing thirty songs with an interval between the two halves. The applause after "Till" was longer than the song itself, but what sent the audience frantic was her *Irony of War* medley towards the end of her recital. Dot had placed it here she said in case she was booed. She had not performed to a capacity audience, having sold just 1,700 of the 2,800 seats, but even this was an achievement for a non-classical artiste, and after her final song, she returned to the stage after one last curtain-call and told the audience, "The next time I come here I'll fill this place!"

Mayor John Lindsay's telegram read: "Congratulations, Dorothy, for bringing New Yorkers a Night To Remember."

American journalists, like their British counterparts had shortish memories if an artiste had not graced their concert

133

platforms or the record charts for a while. Therefore the question frequently posed was, "*Who* is Dorothy Squires?" The *Los Angeles Times*' Mary Murphy met Dot after the show and, having heard of her reputation was bowled over by her charm:

> Who is Dorothy Squires? It's difficult to describe her without gushing. But one might think we, at the Music Center, were being paid off. Since this is not the case, let's gush. It is the incredible optimism and enthusiasm of this woman that strikes you first. It's the soul in her voice when you listen to her album. It's the way she looks directly into your eyes, whether you ask her tough or bland questions or not. But she touches most deeply with her warmth and piercing honesty.

Two days before the concert she had told Gregg Hunter of the *Glendale News-Press*:

> This is the most expensive paid-for audition in history but please don't get the notion that I'm on some sort of ego trip because I like to hear myself sing. Should I lose thousands on the venture, it's worth every penny to make friends here."

The columnist Ivy Crane Wilson had a few years earlier wanted to include "Happy Newlyweds Dorothy And Roger" in one of her famous *Hollywood Albums*, but Dot had refused to entertain the idea. Wilson had obviously forgiven her the snub and now observed:

> They cheered and applauded as Dot belted out a three-hour programme of her favourite songs and nostalgic anecdotes. It seemed like the entire audience was at the sumptuous party afterwards.

134

Patricia O'Haire, The *New York Daily News'* frequently acerbic show business reporter, enthused:

> When it comes to being a gambler, Dorothy Squires has to be ranked up there with Nick the Greek or maybe even Sky Masterson. She is certainly a classic example of the old gambler's expression of "putting her money where her mouth is". Okay, so you've never heard of Dorothy Squires? That's nothing to be ashamed of. Matter of fact, hardly anyone outside her native turf, which happens to be England, has heard much about her. But that's a condition Dorothy Squires has set about to change. I must say—watching her perform at Carnegie—I had to be impressed with her onstage presence. She has warmth, wit and confidence, and she also has a voice that is several decibels louder than Tom Jones and Engelbert Humperdinck combined.

Billboard applauded Richard Armitage's suggestion that other major European stars, not known outside their own countries, should follow Dot's example:

> European artists solidly entrenched in their own markets and who have proven their ability to draw audiences should emulate UK singer Dorothy Squires, who booked the 2,785-seat Carnegie Hall for one concert only, said her manager. He considers the cost of the concert—plus one other at the Los Angeles Music Center—cheap at the price in terms of publicity and public reaction....Armitage admitted that there was no way that the two concerts could make money for her, even if the two halls were one-hundred per cent full, and adds, "Before the start, we knew we'd be down financially, but as I said, it isn't a gamble, it's an investment.

135

Armitage gave *Billboard* a typed statement to be included in their feature, claiming that he had written this on Dot's behalf. In fact, the statement had been composed in the third person and as an act of self-commendation by Dot herself:

> There are major artists in Europe—such as Cliff Richard in the UK and Sylvie Vartan in France—who mean very little to the huge US market. It should be possible for these proven artists to do the same thing as Dorothy—book major venues themselves and open up a new market with their own money. It's no good waiting around to get a hit record and then ride on that—and you can't just sneak into a major market like New York. In times of advance publicity and advertising on radio and in the press—and at the event itself, Dorothy Squires has established herself as an entity in New York show business. We treat the money spent on the project as research and development expenses.

Backstage at Carnegie Hall, Dot had been introduced to the singer-songwriter-poet Rod McKuen, who presented her with a song which he said he had written especially for her. She recalled:

> From the moment we met, he called me Dotty. He said he'd been a fan of mine for many years, and added that he had written this song just for me, words and music, upon hearing that I was coming back to America. This was 'Solitude's My Home'. No one since Billy Reid—certainly of that calibre—had written especially for me. I was so touched that I cried on his shoulder.

McKuen (1933-2015) was feted for his English adaptations

of the works of his friend, Belgian singer Jacques Brel. Indeed, there are few modern-day singers worthy of their salt who have *not* sung at least one of these, most especially "If You Go Away" ("Ne me quitte pas") and "If We Only Have Love" ("Quand on n'a que l'amour"). Dot was very much mistaken however in thinking that McKuen had written the words *and* music to "Solitude's My Home", let alone that he had done this for her. The original had been written and composed in 1966 by Georges Moustaki (who wrote Edith Piaf's "Milord", amongst others) as "Ma solitude", and given to Serge Reggiani who had a massive hit with it in France. McKuen *had* written the English lyrics, for himself, and Dot's record company risked being sued by only having *his* name in the credits and not Moustaki's. When I tried pointing this out to Dot, she argued that *I* had made a mistake, so I left it at that!

Dot's American concerts gave Robert Nesbitt an excuse, she claimed, to inform her that she *would* have been invited to top the bill in that year's Royal Variety Show—to be recorded at the Palladium on 30 October and broadcast the following week, *had* she been free to appear.

"That slimy sod would never have been able to lie straight in bed," was her response. "And did you see who he replaced me with? Carol-fucking-Channing, if Danny La Rue wasn't bad enough!"

Dot and La Rue had been friends for years, but she and many of her fans found it hard to forgive him, or Douglas Darnell, for the finale of this show. Wearing a replica of one of her gowns made especially for the occasion by Darnell, La Rue strode on to the stage and sent her up with a truly *gross* parody of "Say It With Flowers" and "My Way".

"Danny told me it was all his own idea," she said. "I didn't believe that for one minute. Robert Nesbitt put him up to it to get back at me, I was sure of it. I wanted to forgive Danny because he was apologetic afterwards, but it was all an act. They'd conspired together, the bastards."

On 25 November 1972, Dot appeared on ITV's *The Russell Harty Show,* her first television chat show interview since two appearances on *Frost on Sunday* in October and November 1968. Blackburn-born Harty (1934-88) was not exactly subtle in his approach, in the days when chat show hosts did not feel obliged to rely on "idiot cards". He does not do too badly here, though his interview with Dot a few years later would see her getting hot under the collar, and his rudeness whilst interviewing the singer Grace Jones in 1980 would see her belting him over the head! Dot took up most of the show—23 minutes—opening the proceedings with "Till". Halfway through, she sang "If I Could Go Back", of which more later, and closed with "The Man That Got Away", and a reprise of "My Way". Harty began by asking her the question she had been asked many times before. Why was she booking theatres herself instead of having someone do it for her?

"At first nobody would, now I won't let them," she all but spat at him, though so far in a friendly manner.

And when asked to describe the "Squires phenomenon" she replied, "All the world loves a fighter...God helps them that help themselves."

For once, Dot had a good word to say about the "moguls": Lew and Leslie Grade, and Bernard Delfont, saying that as Jewish emigrés they had started off with nothing, and that they did not always know what was going on in "the office next door". She was obviously referring to Robert Nesbitt.

"There were two men I hated more than any others in the world—Nesbitt and Murdoch," she told me. "They each in their own way tried to destroy me—one putting in his spoke to stop me working for the BBC, the other with all the shit that was printed about me in the *News of the World* at the time of the Janie Jones thing."

Harty then touched on a sore point, asking her how it had felt—sitting in her luxurious home, with no work to go to and waiting for the phone to ring. He even had the nerve to ask her, half-joking, if she had drank or taken drugs.

"No, I didn't drink," she snarled, glancing off-stage into the wings at Nicky Welsh, who later said that he had expected her to get up and walk off the set. "Do me a favour. The cops thought I did!"

Dot then changed the subject, and spoke about the musical version of *Sunset Boulevard*, which she had discussed during a recent trip to Hollywood—she said that this would be opening in the West End in September 1973, with her in the central role of Norma Desmond, whilst Bette Davis would be opening on the same night on Broadway. However, when Harty asked for more details of this, she changed the subject again and began discussing *Old Rowley*. Sarah Miles was Harty's other guest on the show: her husband Robert Bolt had written the screenplay for *A Man For All Seasons*, in which Paul Schofield had portrayed Sir Thomas More. Dot said that she had met her backstage, but that she had not got around to telling her that if she could persuade her husband to script *Old Rowley*, and engage Schofield to play Charles II, then she herself would play Nell Gwynne!

"If it's the last thing I do on this earth, I'm going to get this score to Robert Bolt," she exclaimed.

Minutes later, the interview was interrupted when Miles clomped on to the set, informed Dot that she had just spoken to Bolt on the phone—and that he *would* write the script, but only if *he* could play the Merry Monarch! Miles then dashed off, and Harty began grilling Dot once more, telling her how surprised he was that, if her joviality tonight was anything to go by, she had obviously got over Roger Moore. Knowing her as well as I did whenever the subject was brought up, I was surprised at her calm response:

> I'm very lucky that I'm able to be in this frame of mind. For the first two or three years it was pretty rough. The worst thing of all is the sense of being inadequate saying, "Where did I go wrong?" It gave

139

me a terrible sense of insecurity. So I thought, "Well, I'll show him." And that's what I did.

But, Harty pressed, as if he had not pushed his luck already, was she *still* in love with Moore? Again, she kept her cool:

> No, no! You can never love anybody or anything that you've lost respect for. But, may I say this. Roger was a knockout guy and I wish him all the luck in the world, because I had nine years with Roger that many women never have in their whole lifetimes. I wish that I could tell all females that, whose husbands have left them, "Don't ever feel bitter about it!"

"Solitude's My Home" was one of the highlights of Dot's third recorded Palladium recital the next evening. Allegedly, because George Moustaki's name was not included in the songwriting credits on the album, as with the single—and because Dot still refused to acknowledge that *he* had introduced the song and that it had not been created *just* for her—Moustaki made such a fuss that *Palladium 1972* remains one of the two Dorothy Squires albums not to have been re-released on compact disc. This is a pity, for there are some quite electrifying moments here—from the light-hearted "I Only Wanna Laugh", by way of Hoagy Carmichael's "Stardust", and concluding with Burt Bacharach's and Hal David's high-powered theme from *Lost Horizon*, "If I Could Go Back". In the film the song was lip-synched by Peter Finch (to the voice of Jerry Whitman, whose wife, Diane Lee, provided the singing voice for Finch's co-star in the film, Liv Ullman), and there was a cover version by Andy Williams. Dot, however, pulls out all the stops and hits some formidably high, elongated notes, therefore her reading of the number may be defined as definitive. I was once sitting on the front row on the tour circuit when she dislocated her jaw whilst singing it—no problem, for she retired to the wings, and strode back on a few minutes later to resume her set as if nothing had happened! She told Sally Clyde, after this third Palladium:

> You can't imagine how many impresarios would like to back my concerts. But I wouldn't dream of it. I've proved that I can attract an audience. Now I can take my choice. And I prefer to do it my way. I don't want anyone else to handle me. I like to be in control of the various facets that make up a production. I've reached an earning capacity where I can afford to promote my concerts and, more importantly, to promote them precisely as I want them. I'm a gambler. I always have been.

A few days after the Palladium, Dot taped a guest slot for *The Reg Varney Christmas Revue*, broadcast on 23 December. The Osmonds also appeared on the bill, but it was Dot who received the wildest applause. On a minimalistic set and looking stunning in a shell-pink Douglas Darnell gown she sang "If I Could Go Back" her one-off single for the Bell label backed by her own "As The Saying Goes". In January 1973 she hit the roof on reading an interview given in London by Roger Moore and Luisa Mattioli to an American reporter—the occasion being his having been contracted, the previous August, to play James Bond in *Live And Let Die*. The syndicated feature had headlined newspaper supplements across America at the beginning of the month. Moore as usual had only spoken kindly about Dot. Not so Ms. Mattioli, whose rant had been published as it had been spoken, in broken English. Dot was quoted as having said, though the reporter did not say to whom, and when:

> I know I must have appeared stonyhearted in refusing so long to divorce him. But I had a big, big

141

heartache I was carrying around with me. I was stubbornly determined that the woman who had taken Roger from me would never, never become his wife. But I guess time heals all wounds and the bitterness fades with the years. I never expected Roger to be completely faithful...As handsome as he was, the girls were always chasing him. But I simply blocked those thoughts from my mind. What one doesn't know doesn't hurt one. But I'm no longer bitter or filled with recrimination. I wish him the best of luck.

In her interview, Luisa explained how she had argued with her parents who disapproved of her living with Moore and having children out of wedlock. She added that such was their anger that she had convinced them not to harm him, and that if they were patient, Moore *would* marry her. She then explained how and when she and the man with "no vinegar in his nature" had fallen in love, and what had happened afterwards:

> He told his wife, Dorothy Squires, a very popular singer here, and like a decent, respectable man, he asked for a divorce. His wife said no. For eight years, this woman, this Dorothy Squires, would not divorce Roger. She is many years older than he is. She thought his love for me was infatuation—that it would pass. And of course she was jealous. And I could understand that. She practiced—how do you call it?—self-delusion. Even after our children were born, even after Roger and I set up house, she still would not divorce. It was very difficult for us. You can imagine. Difficult for me, for my family in Italy, for the children. And of course, for Roger. No interviews. Nothing about his private life. No pictures of me, the children. Lies, whispers, gossips. I was living somewhere between heaven and hell, always

under a cloud. After five, six years, I tell you the truth. "She will never give you a divorce," I tell Roger. But he says, "Don't give up hoping." Then one day, November 1968, Dorothy Squires, I never see her. We have never met. One day she charged Roger with desertion, and she gets the divorce. I could not believe it. I think now it was because of her friends. They told her she was being silly, mean, revenge. What for? Roger was not coming back to her, Never. I think she realised that.

Bringing Luisa's name up in a conversation was akin to walking across a minefield, unless Dot broached the subject first. She *had* by now forgiven Moore for leaving her—as she says, she had expected this all along because, handsome as he was, in his line of work the temptation had always been there.

"Anyone else, I would have eventually accepted," she told me, when the news broke that the couple had split. "But not the Italian. I'm glad he eventually left her."

On the plus side, Dot made some headway with the BBC when, beginning on 19 March, she became Radio Two's Star For A Week. This saw her records being played on *every* show, along with a 60-minute concert recorded in Manchester especially for the event. For reasons known only to herself, Dot insisted there should be *no* Billy Reid songs, and also left out "For Once In My Life" and "Till".

"Oh, my heavens," she had told Margaret Pride, on the eve of the concert. "I've said some pretty rude things about the BBC in my time, but I take them all back. I think the BBC are marvellous. Absolutely super!"

Pride had been invited to Dot's Bexley home to interview her, and though warned of the consequences should she catch her subject in a spiky mood, the split from Roger Moore and its aftermath was at the top of the journalist's agenda, even after twelve years. Pride asked her if she would marry again. She responded calmly, to the one question that even her closest friends might not have dared put to her:

> No, I wouldn't. Not again. I've had boyfriends, of course, and I'd live with a man. But no marriage. If a woman is married, and deserted, it gives her a terrible feeling of inferiority. I still feel very insecure. Money? It's absolutely no bloody use at a time of emotional distress. To some, I may seem a toughie, and I have this rod of steel in my back. But honestly, I think I'm the easiest touch in the business.

When Pride asked if she ever felt lonely, she replied:

> At home, I am never lonely. Sometimes in a crowded room, or at a party when people think I am having a whale of a time, I can be lonely. But I would never show it. To the public I always try to appear serene and confident. Sadness and loneliness are very private things and should never be inflicted on other people.

Dot's next venture should have been a tour of America—a second show at Carnegie Hall followed by dates in Los Angeles, Chicago, and a number of unspecified venues. This was cancelled in the wake of an interview she gave to Michael Cable of *Easy Listening*, in June 1973. Cable, who described her to his readers as having the reputation of a fire-snorting dragon, was invited to St Mary's Mount, and began his subsequent feature by suggesting that parts of the property were in a state of disrepair:

> The extensive grounds include a swimming pool, half empty and with the flotsam of winter making it marginally less inviting than a Florida swamp—a gaily painted tinker's caravan (a gift from a fan) and

144

a general air of being ready to scream at the mere sight of a fork. Clearly the owner's interests do not extend to gardening.

Dot was displeased to read this, but even angrier because Cable had published her comments about Americans, under the headline on the magazine cover, "Americans Are Bastards To British Artists"—claiming that she had made these in confidence and not to be repeated. These gave Richard Armitage considerable cause for concern:

> I knew [the States] wasn't going to be a picnic because I'm virtually unknown there. Maybe I was being a bit over-ambitious, but I said I was going to go there and when I say I'm going to do something, I do it....Had I known what I was up against, I probably would not have gone but even so I'm glad I did. It put a hallmark on me, and I have had a lot of offers from America as a result. I just wish I could reverse our treatment of Americans. We are very good to them. They are not nearly as good to us. Over here any bloody idiot who speaks with an American accent is treated like a bloody god, which is terribly unfair. In return the Americans are bastards to English artists. They won't let anybody in, and when they do they nail you to the bloody cross.

Just days after the interview was published, Richard Armitage contacted Dot to inform her that the tour had been called off and that the chances of her ever performing again in America were now virtually nil. Dot merely shrugged her shoulders, and put it about that *she* had eschewed the tour—for a week-long engagement at a small venue in Llanelli is not known. An advertisement heralding the event appeared in the *Llanelli Star*.

145

Dorothy Squires Cancels American Tour To Appear In Her Own Town With Nicky Welsh & His Orchestra. Book Now To Avoid Disappointment. Hurry. Hurry. Hurry.

She had been booked for eight performances at the recently opened Cabaret Candlelight nightclub, the first to take place on 1 October. After hugging relatives and friends, she told reporters who gathered around her car after she had parked it outside a friend's home:

> I'm bringing my Drury Lane premiere home. I'm also bringing Dennis Lotis, together with my musical director Nicky Welsh, pianist Kenny Brown and drummer Mac Swan to Llanelli. We will be trying out several ideas for Drury Lane. I'm thinking of adding an Ivor Novello medley instead of the autograph sequence I usually have. And may I say how nice it is to be back here in the place that I call home!

"I meant that," she said. "I've always been proud of my roots. I've never ruled out going back to live in my home town of Llanelli if God forbid everything ever goes arse-up."

She was amused, too, that the club had formerly been a police station—and her dressing room a holding-cell which still had bars up at one of the windows!

"I really *was* at home," she chuckled. "And for once they didn't lock me in!"

Dot had hired the Theatre Royal for a concert on 9 December, to be recorded and released on a double album so the Llanelli shows were extended dress-rehearsals to try out new material, as Dot herself confessed. Even so her performances were reported to have been exemplary, with the Deputy Mayor and Mayoress of Llanelli attending every one, though none of the reviews reported *what* she sang. The *Llanelli Star* observed:

Standing on their ears—that's the effect Dorothy Squires is having on Cabaret Candlelight audiences this week. Pontyberem-born Dorothy has become Britain's Miss Show Business in a starry career that has known an overflowing share of heartaches and happiness. And again she has come to Llanelli for early inspiration. It is a self-sponsored week for Queen Dorothy of Old Drury…"I'm always willing to take over a place and work on the profits," she says. "I know my own drawing power and other stars will have to work on the same basis if they will demand high fees." World-travelled Dorothy always jumps at the chance of a visit home and would probably sing for nothing to be back among her own people. "I'm so looking forwards to seeing my relatives and friends. I'll be bringing my sister Rene with me. Every night at the Candlelight is to be a gala night," she promises. And Dorothy Squires is a lady who keeps her word. At Candlelight Cabaret Miss Squires made arrangements for the stage to be extended by twelve feet for her orchestra to be accommodated behind her. And she has been kitted out with her £500 gowns all week—a star-studded romantic with great drawing power, that's our Dot.

Why Dot paired up with Johannesburg-born crooner Lotis, who despite his popularity in the 1950s never enjoyed any chart successes, remained a mystery until she explained:

> I wanted Russ Conway, but he wasn't available at that particular time and in any case he was in a bad shape. He was still getting over the stroke he'd had a few years over, and almost permanently drunk and addicted to pills because his sexuality had almost been exposed by the press. So Nicky Welsh

147

suggested Dennis Lotis, who was down on his luck. I didn't like him at first—more to the point, he'd done something to hurt me in the past—but once we started working together it was forgive and forget and we became friends again, but *not* lovers, as some thought.

Dot's admission that she initially disliked Lotis was very much of an understatement—she had loathed him! Speaking to the *Eastern Daily Press* on the eve of his farewell performance in August 2005 at the Mundesley Festival, held annually in Norfolk where he had lived for some time, Lotis recalled the reason for Dot's resentment:

> I am surprisingly good friends with Roger Moore's ex-wife, Dorothy Squires. We fell out years ago when we were living in Mill Hill and she and Roger had just separated. He had phoned me up to ask me to find him a house near us for him and a young lady called Luisa who he was bringing back from Italy. He was filming *The Saint* at the time, and as the Elstree studios were near Mill Hill it would be a perfect location. But he didn't want Dorothy to know. However, somehow Dorothy did find out and she came along one night and threw bricks at all the windows. Roger phoned me and asked if they could come and stay at our house because Luisa was terrified. After a few nights with us the phone rang and it was Dorothy in vitriolic fashion, going crazy that we had Roger's "Italian cow" at our house. We didn't talk after that night for two years, but then she rang out of the blue to say she had just heard me on the radio and that it was "bloody marvellous" and that we should work together again. We sold out the Drury Lane Theatre and recorded an album so all was definitely forgiven.

The Theatre Royal, Drury Lane was the last time that Dot felt the need to book herself. The evening was billed as "The Dorothy Squires Show", and was exactly this—though as in the past when minor and sometimes virtually unknown artistes were supporting, the audience grew restless and were only really interested in who was topping the bill, and who they had paid to come and see. The musicians were the same as before—the only change being the backing singers, The Coffee Set from her BBC Manchester concert, who introduced her with "She's That Someone", from *Mame*. Fans were surprised, if not a little shocked, when she walked onto the stage—having eschewed one of her Douglas Darnell gowns for an olive riding suit, the skirt of which was split to the hip, and wearing a plumed top hat. She had, she told the press, always dreamed of playing the title-role in *Mame*, and to prove this point performed several numbers from the show. Her version of "If He Walked Into My Life" is in a class of its own whilst Kenny Brown's "Who Else But Me" and Dot's powerhouse reading of "Something Greater", from the musical, *Applause*, bring a lump to the throat. Indeed, the only weak point in the first half of the recital is her duet with 14-year-old boy soprano, Michael Ward—a ditty entitled "You're My Best Girl", this was embarrassing to watch.

After the interval Dot returned to the stage, "reunited" with her Darnell gown. She opened with Cy Coleman and Dorothy Fields' "Nobody Does It Like Me", which she embellished with a few lyrics of her own, hitting out at the trials and tribulations of the last two years. This ran into the bouncy "On The Sunny Side of the Street", after which Dot performed her *Young Men With Heads On High Soliloquy*, one of the most portentous sequences of her career. Every bit as intense and moving as her earlier *Irony of War* segment, this included "Danny Boy", "The Whiffenpoof Song", and the soliloquy title. Sitting on the floor of the stage, this was the only time I had ever seen her actually *hold* a microphone, as opposed to performing the way Piaf and Dietrich had, standing behind it on the stage, moving only her arms and hands. Then, after Sammy Cahn's "Until The Real Thing Comes Along" and her own "Eyes Of A Man", she went into her *Show Tunes* sequence—having decided at the last minute *not* to perform any Novello songs, she thrilled with "Some Enchanted Evening", "Hello, Young Lovers", and "I Could Have Danced All Night", before rounding off with "Heart Of A City" from the still un-produced *Old Rowley*, and "Climb Every Mountain" from *The Sound Of Music*. And the *big* surprise, or indeed shock of the evening—Dot did *not* sing "My Way".

The writers of "Nobody Does It Like Me" were not impressed by the way Dot had "mucked around" with their lyrics—kicking up such a fuss that the album was withdrawn within weeks of its release and the "offending" song removed. Dot however did not want the fans to be cheated, so she bought all the available copies of the original album and handed them over to me—so that my wife and I could sell them in theatre foyers before her future shows!

Early in 1974, Dot and Dennis Lotis recorded eleven solos and duets for an autobiographical concept album which she entitled, *Cheese 'n' Wine*. She penned the sleeve-notes, part of which read:

> An unexpected guest did sit down and dine. That unexpected guest was my husband. The marriage was to last ten years, and like most things in life it didn't last, but then again nothing lasts for ever. When one loses a loved one, be it to another love, or even to death itself, life still has to go on....You can fall in love again, maybe not as fervently as your first love, but fall in love you will, and when you least expect it. I sincerely hope that when you play this record, and understand the message we've tried to convey, you will again lift up your head and say, "Tomorrow is another day."

150

Cheese 'n' Wine is the only Dorothy Squires studio album not to have been released on compact disc, allegedly because she was sharing the titular honours with someone else that the fans might not have been interested in.

"Many Squires fans would buy the CD, that's for sure," a record company executive told me. "However, many more would not because effectively they be paying for an album but getting only half of one if they weren't interested in Dennis Lotis, whose records just didn't sell, certainly not to warrant releasing them on a mid or full-price CD."

Fans that I spoke to during the subsequent tour attested to the fact that singing with someone else weakened the Squires voice considerably, and thus prevented her from "letting rip", which was why there had been so few duets in the past. Also, the fact that this was a concept album, with these songs focusing on the Squires-Moore story, but performed with a "stand-in", so to speak, resulted in an uncomfortable mix of schmaltz, high-camp and acute embarrassment. There were many arguments backstage, before and after the shows, between Dot and her retinue—some of whom could not stand Dennis Lotis. I was witness to one very vocal incident between one musician and Doris Gaard, who was asked to go into Dot's dressing-room and give her an ultimatum: that she should get shot of Lotis, or the musician would walk!

"He was a B-list crooner who'd seen better days," Johnnie Gray said, confirming that others had also threatened to leave Dot's entourage unless Lotis went. "Yet the way he lorded it over everyone, you would think he was Frank-bloody-Sinatra. On one occasion, some of them got so upset that they headed for the bar during the interval and didn't come back on stage until Dot was half-way through her first song."

The occasion was Dot's concert in Chatham, witnessed by Linda Rogers of the *Chatham Daily News*. In her not so very flattering feature, "Dot And Her Two-Fingered Grand Exit", she observed:

151

I went to the Dorothy Squires Show at Chatham's Central Hall on Friday prepared to admire professional showmanship from someone who, they tell me, has been thrilling audiences since before I was born. And I came away feeling slightly embarrassed by it all. I was quite happy until the interval...Dennis Lotis followed and went through a fairly predictable repertoire of Tony Bennett/Bobby Darin-type songs, interspersed with a little soft-shoe shuffling. This left him rather short of breath and I suspect that age is catching up. The second part of the show began badly as three members of the orchestra arrived halfway through the first number....Miss Squires has still the ability and energy to give a highly emotional performance and to tug at heart-strings, if you happen to be susceptible to that kind of act. But musically her voice needs all the help that a recording studio can give it...she was even out of time with the orchestra during "For Once In My Life". But the audience was an indulgent one and shouts of "Don't worry Dot" and "Keep it up, girl, we still love you" met the cracks in her voice and the forgotten words. Obviously it was a performance to be enjoyed by a retrospective audience who could remember Miss Squires from her heyday. But from the point of view of someone who has not seen that past, and all that was left was the self-indulgence which showed itself not only in the presentation, but also in the songs she has written recently. One particularly painful example was a rendering of "Three Little Lambs". [she meant "The Whippenpoof Song"]. I think they should just let her retire in peace, and just admire the defiant gesture of an embittered star who feels she has been cold-shouldered by the media and is determined to make a spectacular, two-fingered exit.

152

Dot always took such negative reviews to heart, though eventually she saw them for what they were—journalists who could be spiteful for being spiteful's sake:

> Some people come to my shows *only* with the intention of giving me a bad review, whether I've performed well or not. It's usually the ones who get complimentary tickets. The fans have always taken the rough with the smooth, and they never complain!

Cheese And Wine did not sell nearly as Dot's other albums and she wisely called it a day with Dennis Lotis to concentrate on what she did best—wearing her heart on her sleeve, standing alone in the middle of the stage.

Carnegie Hall, October 1972

154

At Llanelli's Candlelight Cabaret
with manager Don Bates and the
Deputy Mayor and Mayoress

In her *Mame* costume for her Drury
Lane premiere…in Llanelli!

On holiday in Iceland, 1974.

10: Catfights & Plumes

"She's been called outrageous, dangerous, big-headed, giant-sized, super-colossal. She's not to be put down, ignored or ever forgotten. She is Dorothy Squires. Russell Harty.

1974 was a year of mixed fortunes: triumphs and tragedies in equal measure. Dot gave her only ever interview to the British pop press, when Tony Stewart of the *New Musical Express* turned up backstage after a show in Margate.

"I must have been bloody crackers," she told me. "Since when did those sort of journalists ever have any respect for anyone? And did you see the title of that piece? I could have throttled him!"

Stewart headed his feature, "Dot, Pot, And Growing Old Gracefully", and confessed to being terrified of meeting her, observing, "Esteemed music biz people have actually been witnessed to tremble violently with fear and cower under their desks at the mere mention of her name."

Neither was he flattering towards her when, after enthusing about her "chic ensemble of leopard skin patterned blouse and shirt—and thick woollen gloves, he added, "The wrinkles are now creeping like caterpillars across her brow, mouth and neck, and she showed obvious signs of middle-aged spread. But she fights it off."

But if Stewart was too timid—or cowardly—to say this to Dot's face, she did not hold back when telling him off about *his* appearance.

"He was a scruffy bugger," she said. "He was wearing a dirty T-shirt, and a good wash wouldn't have hurt him."

Neither did she mince her words when discussing modern day pop stars:

> When I see some of these acts on stage today they appall me. I think they're bloody disgusting. We are

in *show business*—an escape for the audience. And it's a very glamorous business. If people go to see you, the least you can do is take them away from the humdrum problems they have—their rates [council tax], their taxes or can-they-get-any-pot-or-not....It's very sad when you see somebody come along with all this bloody glitter and painted faces. Christ, I wonder what the hell we're coming to? *What* is it all about? You can't call *them* stars. I don't really know how to differentiate between what is and what isn't a star—but that phase certainly won't last. How many have you seen go by the wayside? You say, "Oh, Christ, who *was* that? He was big at one time when he had his hair green. Can you name me a female or male star that's likely to last? Can you name me *any*? I'm buggered if I can!

Regarding comments made in the tabloids about her "busy" love-life, she scathed:

They think my life has been in and out of bed with every man you ever saw. I wish to Christ it was. If you're a nymphomaniac you can't get hurt, but I have to dig a guy very much before I jump in the sack. Sometimes I envy nymphomaniacs, but they think *I'm* a bloody nymphomaniac. Whether it's my drummer, my trainer or anybody, they say, "Oh, Christ, I bet she's having it off there." But it never happens. It would never happen with somebody I employ. That you *can't* have. And secondly, again, I have to dig somebody a great deal.

Dot *was* in a relationship, and had been for over a year. "Tom" (not his real name) was twenty years her junior, recently divorced, and though not as handsome as Roger Moore had been always treated her kindly and, so far as is known never cheated on her. They also had something in common—a ferocious temper. I once saw Tom lose it big time, back stage with a journalist who made a comment about Dot that he might have been better keeping to himself.

The "age thing" cropped up on 25 March, when invitations were sent out to Dot's friends for a "50th Birthday Bash" backstage at the 2,300-seater Liverpool Empire. She was of course as much as nine years older than this, depending upon which account of her birth one wishes to heed. This was a Monday evening and she had hired the theatre for the whole week, with all the tickets sold before curtain-up of the premiere. To say the event was crazy may be an understatement. Pianist Mike Terry and Dennis Lotis were supporting, and all around us we could hear people mumbling for them to hurry up and get off. Dot was on stage for *three* hours, with just a fifteen-minute interval which saw virtually no one leaving their seats. She opened with "Nobody Does It Like Me", and had a fit of giggles when she slipped up with one of the lines, arguably on purpose, belting out, "If there's a problem, I duck it...I don't solve it, I just fuck it up!" The audience roared with laughter. Then, after "Say It With Flowers" there was a ten-minutes hiatus whilst dozens of fans and friends—my wife and I amongst them—filed onto the stage to pay homage and "worship at the shrine of Saint Dot" with our bouquets and birthday gifts, so many that it was virtually impossible to walk off without standing on them.

After the show, for which Dot gave five curtain calls and received a twenty-minutes standing ovation, we headed for her dressing-room. An hour later, were having one of our "car chats" with me sitting atop Dot's "new baby"—a spanking new Chrysler, her birthday present to herself. Then we were joined by Tom, who had arranged a party at a nearby club, and which raged until three in the morning.

Later in the year, Dot almost lost her life when her house caught fire, during the early hours of the morning. A

159

dozen people were sleeping in the property: her sister Renee, friends and fans staying the night, others renting rooms. David Pope rescued Dot from the blaze—oblivious to what was happening because she had taken sleeping tablets. In her memoirs she recalls coming to, and groggily crawling along the passage outside her bedroom, trying to find the stairs whilst the smoke was suffocating her—falling halfway down them, and snagging her foot in the banister rails and hanging helplessly until Pope burst through the door, in his haste tripping on his way up the stairs and landing on top of her, knocking her unconscious. Before escaping from her bedroom, Dot had managed to grab her jewel case and a casket containing 400 of Roger Moore's love-letters. The press, who since the Payola scandal had had an axe to grind, made much of this. She then started panicking because her dogs—Jason and Esban, the latter named after her horse—were still in the building. Esban was saved, but Jason, her standard poodle, suffocated and died. The press had arrived on the scene at the same time as the fire-brigade, and photographers tripped over one another to get a picture of a scorched and blackened and very distressed Dot, sitting on the lawn whilst being comforted by friends, with Esban crouched at her feet.

Because the house was under-insured, she lost a fortune. The tragedy so affected her that she was compelled to spend several weeks recuperating in a private nursing home, after which she stayed with friends. Subsequently she relocated to North Wing, a 17-room riverside mansion on Fishery Road in Bray, Berkshire, which had once belonged to Edward VII's mistress, Lily Langtry. Here her near neighbours were Terry Wogan, Michael Parkinson, and our mutual friend Marion Montgomery who remembered:

> Dorothy was in a dreadful state. Her dogs like her horses were her whole life. For her, losing one was like losing a child. She was inconsolable. I had last

seen her looking glamorous in one of those beautiful gowns and dripping with jewels. When Tom brought her to my house for dinner, I scarcely recognised her. She really did look like a little old lady. She stayed with me for a few days, and I would like to think I cheered her up. The next time I saw her she was back to her old laughing, cursing, hell-playing self. But I'm certain that deep inside she was still suffering.

Tragedy struck again when North Wing became flooded after the Thames burst its banks during adverse weather conditions, and Dot had to leave the property in a boat. Despite the storm, the press were quickly on the scene and as before published only the most distressing pictures.

On the plus side, Dot enjoyed tremendous success with her racehorses. She started with a third-share in Spuronia, whose father Larkspur won the 1962 Derby. Fair Gazette was trained by Paddy Murphy in Ireland. Esban, Knockulin, Walberswick and Norwegian Flag were with David Nicholson in Stow-on-the-Wold. The latter had won at Leopardstown in February 1971. Esban had won the 1973 Scottish Grand National. Now she was hoping for big things with May I Say, named after one of her favourite phrases and trained by David Jermy, at Carshalton. In her memoirs she recalls the horse her father bought in to pull his cart. Archie had set off for the horse fair intent on spending no more than £20 on an "old nag to do the job", but had paid £80 for Dolly, the mare who had subsequently become a family pet. Dot likewise had flown to an auction in Dublin, expecting to buy a decent National Hunt horse for £5,000—but instead had forked out £10,000 for Esban, a beautiful gelding. She told The Star's Charles Croft:

> My Esban always has a dab of lipstick on his nose when he runs. He recognises my perfume, 'Joy'. It's a very expensive perfume, and I never have to buy

any. My fans keep me supplied, God bless 'em! I kiss all my horses, who know me from my visits to the training yard. Racing is the first priority of my life, and I pick my theatre bookings to be as near as possible where they run. I love National Hunt. There is no greater thrill in the world than to see your colours carried past the winning post, with the horse trying with all its heart, and they know when they have won. I make a fuss of them whether they win or not.

Dot was Number Twelve in the National Hunt owners, one place behind the Queen Mother. She enthused:

Esban is one of the best chasers in the game up to four miles. But he is not an Aintree horse, and I would not run him there. I have the same feeling about Esban and Aintree as Anne, Duchess of Westminster had about her great horse Arkle. I am appalled at some owners who run horses in the National when they are not suitable. On the other hand, Norwegian Flag is the ideal Aintree type. I think he would have won the 1975 Grand National but for bruising a tendon and having to miss the race. Now he is just the right age, and will take a lot of beating in the forthcoming National. Remember him on the day!

In 1975, Esban would be transferred across to the stables of her friend, Jenny Pitman, who observed in her memoirs:

Dorothy was an amazing person, almost two personalities. At our home she'd be quite ordinary and as interesting as anybody, but at the racetrack she was pure showbiz: loud and frankly a bit embarrassing. The best horse she sent me was Esban, a nice old grey gelding who at twelve was in

162

the twilight of his career. Even so, we managed to win the Crudwell Cup, a famous race at Warwick, in March 1976....The victory produced a truly dramatic performance from Dot, who hurtled down the track to greet her horse as he came in—with her arms outstretched, like an actress in one of those slow-motion movie embraces. Esban and Aly [Branford, the jockey who rode him] were duly covered in kisses as was anyone else within a fifty-yard radius. "Dot," I thought. "You are quite a case!"

Dot proved herself "quite a case", during her second appearance on *The Russell Harty Show* on 10 January 1975 when the pair crossed swords within a moment of her taking her seat. If she tried to disguise her contempt of Harty with jocular banter she later denounced him as "a slimy little shit" and declared she would never appear on his show again "for all the money in Christendom".

Harty introduced her by telling his audience that Dot was leaving Britain and going to Australia because of all the backstage gossip.

She later told me, "What I *said* was that I was *probably* going to Australia to do a couple of shows, and that I was so pissed off with what the press were writing about me, I might not bother coming back. Harty took my comments seriously. He was never the brightest button in the box."

"You were wrong about the backstage gossip, *very* wrong," she remonstrated to the host. "If I told you *why* I was quitting, we'd close the network."

She was referring to the hate-mail she has received after the Payola scandal, not from the general public but from those who should have known better, celebrities who had a great deal to hide and who had been terrified of being "outed" during the investigation.

Harty would not let up, as Dot stared in disbelief as he edged the flame just that little bit closer to the powder-keg:

163

Are you sure you're not going to Australia in a fit of pique? Are you sure you're not acting over-compulsively? In a sense, don't you *enjoy* things happening to you? I mean, they happen to you at such an alarming and frequent rate. Certain people must be asking themselves, "Does she really enjoy things happening to her? Wouldn't she be depressed if they weren't?

Dot nodded at the table in front of her, then looked at him and said, "You know, it's a good job that I love you very much, because I would have belted you with that bottle for saying that. Do I *love* it? Isn't *that* something! Are you honestly serious about that—that I would be *depressed*?"

Harty changed tactics slightly and now asked her if a *quiet life* would depress her.

"I'd *love* a quiet life," she yelled. "To go to the races, drive up there and see my horses. Do you know, the only time I've been on television is when my horse have won? I haven't done television for the BBC in ten years."

Harty would not learn his lesson, and quipped, "You do have a facility for landing yourself in trouble."

By now, a security man was standing in the wings ready to drag Dot off, for she really did look like she was going to lash out at her host.

"No I don't," she yelled. "Damn it, I wouldn't care if I did. I move to Bray, and I fall in the river the first day I'm there!"

This brought a titter from the audience, and caused Harty to once more change his approach. He asked Dot if she believed in God, and if she ever prayed. She said that she did, but that she never went to church, adding that she had turned to God in 1961 after Roger Moore had left her, and after the death of her father because there had been no one else to turn to. Then Harty asked her if she felt that the time had come to fall in love again and find a shoulder to cry on. One assumes he knew nothing about Tom, who had driven her to the studio.

Momentarily calm she responded, "Actually, I'm afraid because I had it all. In other words, if *that* love that I had for nine and a half years wasn't going to last, nothing would. It's as simple as that."

"Roger Moore," Harty muttered under his breath.

Dot snarled her hackles raised once more, "Why are you mentioning him? You never mentioned me when he was with you last week. Saints alive!"

Moore had appeared on Harty's 20 December show, when the host had dropped a clanger—asking him if he had brought his *real* wife with him this time! Dot brought this up, doubling up with laughter and having the audience in stitches at Harty's expense.

Harty fought back with, "You've mentioned nine and a half years. You've got to mention the *name* of the person you were happy with."

"It could have been somebody else," Dot shot back at him. "I might have had a lover. How do you know? Roger Moore wasn't the only man. Anyway, what I'm trying to say is that I'm scared. I couldn't take that again. You build a wall around you. Once I get involved, I run a mile."

Harty asked if it upset her when people impersonated her—he had obviously heard of her displeasure over Danny La Rue sending her up on the Royal Variety Show. At this she, reconfirmed that La Rue was *still* one of her dearest friends, but launched an attack on Bernard Delfont over comments he had made prior to the 1974 show—not referring to him by name, saying, "He probably owns the network", and offering another clue in that this particular thorn-in-the-side had recently been knighted. She went on:

> He has the audacity to say, "We haven't any female stars in this country to warrant the Command Performance." Mind you, I'd like to be offered it just to say, "Stuff it!" I mean that. I'm never going to have the opportunity because it's become a joke. So—they import Joséphine Baker. I'm not knocking

165

Joséphine Baker, but how do you think the other female stars feeling in this country? How do you think *I* feel?

Dot performed two songs on Harty's show, splendidly arranged by Nicky Welsh. Gordon Jenkins' "This Is All I Ask" had been introduced by Nat King Cole in 1958. Dot had recorded it for Pye, but it had been archived, and instead they released the second song Dot sang tonight as a single: "The Impossible Dream", from *The Man of La Mancha*, with her own "The Eyes Of A Man" on the flipside.

That same month, Dot loaned one of her Douglas Darnell dresses to the comedian Ronnie Corbett to wear for a sketch in *The Two Ronnies*. "*Abdication Street*", which incorporated an emulation of George Formby, was a hilarious send-up of *Coronation Street*.

Dot's unpredictable temperament was brought to the fore in January 1976 when she was invited to appear on ATV Television's *Celebrity Squares*, hosted by Bob Monkhouse. The guests included pianist Mrs. Mills, Lonnie Donegan, John Inman—and Danny La Rue. She had not forgiven La Rue for the Palladium outrage, and told the producers that she would never be seen in any production, even one as frivolous as a game show, alongside a man she had considered a friend, and who had stabbed her in the back by making fun of her in front of millions of people.

There were more fireworks on 8 March when she and the fiery actress Adrienne Corri clashed on Thames TV's, *Take Two*. Broadcast live, the theme was, "Is there *really* no business like show business?" In the interviewer's chair was Llew Gardner, sitting between Dot and Corri. Also present was the *Sunday Mirror*'s show business reporter, Donald Zec, who observed the following week in his feature headed "My Night Out At The Cat Fight":

It was the slanging match of the year, and I told them both—they were like a couple of frisky cats on a hot tin roof. I've now decided this was being unkind to cats. For no self-respecting mog, pedigree or stray, could have matched the loud and unscripted bitchery. Going for each other with forked tongues and blazing eyeballs, they transformed the cheerful *Take Two* chat show into as venomous a clash as you'd find this side of the average snakepit.

According to Zec, in the green room before the show, the two had got along fine—"like nuns at netball"—before turning television into "an abattoir made for two". It was an inebriated Corri who kick-started the rumpus, after Dot announced that if she were to be honest, no one had any *real* friends in show business, and that the only *love* she had in her life was the love she shared with her audiences.

At this, Corri rounded on her with, "Rubbish. Oh, come on. You're only in it for the money and your racehorses!"

Not to be outdone, Dot responded, "Balls! *You're* a phoney. You shouldn't be *in* show business!"

Zec then intervened, politely asking Corri if she had ever attended a Dorothy Squires concert. Corri said that she had not, and the programme went into a premature commercial break whilst Llew Gardner begged his guests to calm down, as this was a live show and there was no contingency plan should the producer pull the plug. When the show came back on, the focus was on the comic, Jim Bowen—Dot's ally in all of this—who castigated Corri, still on stage but off-camera, for picking up a newspaper and ignoring his patter.

"Please don't read while I'm performing," he sniped. "I don't read while *you're* performing. Mind you, I can't find where that is!"

Then the debate resumed, with Dot and Corri addressing the camera as if the other was not there:

DOT: I was bloody furious with Adrienne Corri's attitude to show business....I would have belted her one but I couldn't get near her. I earn £4,000 a week and she gets £200. That's the difference between us."

CORRI: The idea that there is no business like show business is a load of rubbish. It's all an ego trip we get paid for. In any other business we'd get locked up."

And finally, with Corri clearly referring to the Payola scandal and just as it looked like they really *were* going to lay into one another, Llew Gardner stormed off the set, and the credits started to roll!

Liverpool, that "50th"
Birthday bash!

Dot, ripping into the host on *The Russell Harty Show*, 1975.

Signing copies of her album, *Rain, Rain Go Away*, in Llanelli's Falcon Music Shop, 1977.

11: Rain, Rain Go Away!

"I wrote the truth, the whole truth, and nothing but the truth. Unfortunately, some people don't like reading the truth, so the editor kicked up a fuss, saying that parts of the script would have to be amended or removed. I calculated that if I did this, there would be nothing left but the cover." Dorothy Squires.

In the summer of 1971, Dot began dictating her memoirs into the portable tape-recorder she carried around with her and at once—owing to her broadcasting to all and sundry what would be in the finished book—there were threats of lawsuits. Some years later she allowed me to read much of the script. Even some of the chapter headings were litigious, and whilst the sections of the book that I read may legally be paraphrased these titles may not. She also read parts of it over the phone, sometimes with a sob in her voice—more often than not ranting, pretty much as she had during her interview with Ed Moreno. Her book was to be called *Rain, Rain, Go Away*, and she worked on it, off and on, for another five years before sending it to a publisher. She had flatly refused to hire an agent, declaring that they could not always be trusted.

In the introduction, Dot writes of her reputation for being a fighter, a coveted title which she feels she has earned. It was bestowed on her, she adds, when she lay helpless in a corner of life's boxing-ring, her eyes swollen and tear-stained, her arms and legs immobile in the aftermath of her marriage to Roger Moore. The book was accepted by Everest Books, and the serialisation rights sold to the *Sunday People*, who ran them—whilst the script was being frantically edited to remove or "legalise" a reputed 146 litigious statements. Heralding the event, the newspaper proclaimed:

Battling Dorothy Squires has something to sing about again. She has finally won a long legal wrangle for the right to publish her book. Now, at last in the *Sunday People*, she can tell the world of the happiness and the heartache of ten years of marriage to Roger Moore, who now wears the James Bond mantle.

Of her book, she had told the *Sheffield Star's* Jim Greensmith that the title would be either *May I Say* or *What Will I Do For An Encore*, promising, "Nothing will be vitriolic. If it is, it will be with a velvet glove."

During a trip back to Llanelli she gave an interview for Harlech Television and explained:

> The only reason that I wrote the book was to put the record straight. I was so sick of having mud slung at me. I was being smothered by it, and I was so sick of the garbage I was reading, and the things I was hearing. So I just had to get that book out and vindicate myself.

By now the title had been changed to *Rain, Rain Go Away*. Asked why she had chosen this, she explained:

> When I was a kid of about two-and-a-half, all the toilets were out in the garden and were always embellished with beautiful rose trees. And if it was pouring with rain I remember distinctly putting my hand upon the wall and saying, 'Rain, rain, go away—little Nenna wants a pee. And everyone would applaud, even then!

The bone of contention with the script was Dot's inclusion of Roger Moore's love letters to her, and ones to him from Luisa Mattioli that she was accused of intercepting, though this does not appear to have been the case, as they had been delivered to St Mary's Mount, Moore's address at the time. Dot told a press-conference at her home:

Our marriage was an important part of my life, and I can hardly omit it from my autobiography. When he was away on location, Roger used to write to me sometimes three times a day. He wrote some letters in the morning even before he'd cleaned is teeth. I'm quoting from every letter he wrote, but the intimate things I'll be keeping to myself. They were not passionate letters, but beautiful. When my house caught fire, one of the things my secretary and I salvaged were Roger's letters. They were quite intact, though sodden from the firemen's hoses. Wasn't that amazing?

In her last televised interview, Dot was quietly scathing of her bitter rival, saying that there had been four or five letters from Luisa, so illiterate that the sender had been unable to spell the name "Dorothy". One, she said, asked Moore to show the letters to Dot, as proof of their love.

"Now what kind of a cow was that?" she posed.

Moore and Luisa Mattioli took action against her, but the first court hearing was adjourned when it emerged that he was yet to read the script. Two weeks later, Dot was ordered to remove all traces of the letters from her book, and return them to their sender. She complied with the first request but refused to part with the letters because she was not legally obliged to, as Moore had addressed them to her. She was not, however, allowed to discuss them or their content. The *Sun* quoted her as telling one of its journalists:

> I have been living and breathing this book for the last two years. I want to make it quite plain that in no way am I going to lose the respect of the public by writing anything bitter. I am not bitter.

I questioned Dot over this, asking her if she really had spoken to a paper owned by a man, Robert Murdoch, whom she had never stopped despising.

173

"What do you think?" she chortled. "I wouldn't wipe my arse on that fucking rag. As for the letters, I wanted to show the world how much Roger had really loved me, much more than he had ever loved the Italian."

I and her other friends never once heard Dot refer to Luisa Mattioli by her given name. It was always "the Italian", and rarely without an expletive. She next took it upon herself to sue Moore, his wife and Everest Books for preventing publication—and needless to say lost her case. Any lawyer would have told her that copyright of letters belongs to the sender, not to the recipient.

In 1990, after Dot had helped me to find a literary agent—she who had said they could not be trusted!—and my first biography, *The Piaf Legend*, had been published and I had signed the contract for its successor, *The Mistinguett Legend*, she came up with an idea. Now that all else had failed, she suggested that *I* ghost-write her autobiography!

Initially I was happy to do this. I had begun writing *The Great Ladies of Song*, in which I had selected twenty of my favourite singers from around the world, ranging from Peggy Lee to Amália Rodrigues, from Marlene Dietrich to Juliette Gréco. Dot was there under the heading, "The British Bird of Paradise", on account of her colourful costumes. It remains the only script that I have never had published—owing to the claims of my publisher that, not only were some of the women in the book *not* household names, fans of those they admired might not like their idols appearing in the same volume as ones they disliked, pretty much why the *Cheese 'n' Wine* CD had never happened. When I suggested a Dorothy Squires joint autobiographical venture, the response was that she had so rubbed up the establishment the wrong way over the years that I would be hard put to find *any* publisher in Britain willing to take on any such project whilst she was still alive!

"Fuck them," was Dot's response. "I'll find a way."

She never did. She *did* record an album for Decca. Also

entitled *Rain, Rain, Go Away* this was released in 1977, and launched in Llanelli's Falcon Music Shop, where she was mobbed by hundreds of fans. It was voted Middle of the Road Album of the year. Like *Seasons Of...*it was a concept album and autobiographical. It was also self-financed, which enabled Dot to hire one of the best producers in the business: Norman Newell. The sleeve, depicting a portrait of a child replicating little Nenna, looking forlorn whilst watching the rain through her bedroom window, says it all—on the reverse the girl becomes Dorothy Squires, in exactly the same pose.

The album opens with Dot's symphonic composition, "We Clowns", an allegorical take on show business where one puts on a Punchinello mask to hide the pain of braving the slings and arrows of persecutors. Despite the anguish, the applause makes it worthwhile. Dot makes the song effective by keeping it restrained, in the minor key. "Born To Lose" is Norman Newell's English adaptation of Sergio Bardotti's tearjerker, "Aria", the instrumental version of which Acker Bilk had taken to the top of the UK charts. Dot adheres to the original French version, "Aimer avant de mourir", a massive hit on the Continent in 1975 for pop diva, Sheila, in what had been a rare excursion into the world of the tear-jerker, and as such rewards it with the substance that it merits.

Dot's "Megan"—a poem she wrote in 1955 after Freddie Squires' death, and now set to music by Norman Newell, sees her reflecting on the nickname given to her by her brother, who speaks to her from beyond the grave and remembers how he deemed her "wild as the winter hills and fair as daffodils." He recalls how he only wanted the best for her in those far off days and that though they are separated, he says that has never stopped loving her. After Nicky Welsh's new arrangement of "I'll Close My Eyes", her tribute to Billy Reid who had died the previous year, comes Max Steiner's score for the Bette Davis 1942 film *Now Voyager*. Given words by Kim Gannon it had provided the American crooner Dick Haymes with a hit the following year. Dot had wanted to give it less banal and dated lyrics, but was denied this by the Steiner estate, a pity for she would have done a better job than Gannon.

"If I Never Sing Another Song" is possibly the best song on the album—it is certainly the most portentous. It was written by the German singer Alexandra (1942-69), with music by Eurovision Song Contest winner Udo Jurgens. As "Illusionen" it had proved her swansong—just weeks after recording it, Alexandra had been killed in a car accident. Don Black's English lyrics, which like those of "My Way" have nothing in common with the original, nevertheless suit Dot well who, in a slant on "My Way", reflects on a magnificent career where there were accolades galore, and asks herself how she would fare, should it all end. "I would get by," she concludes. "But I don't know how!"

Next up are Jimmy van Heusen's "Here's That Rainy Day", weak by comparison to what one has just heard, and Mel Mitchell's "Passing Strangers"—the latter, arranged by Kenny Brown, sounds much better as a solo than had the duet with Dennis Lotis. Dot then sings Edward Heyman and Victor Young's "Love Letters", formerly a hit for Ketty Lester. Here she refers to Roger Moore's *billet-doux*, salvaged from her blazing home. This incident is directly referred to in her very personal interpretation of Lieber and Stoller's "Is That All There Is?", a US chart-topper for Peggy Lee. With its "Boys And Girls Come Out To Play" introduction, Dot juxtaposes the lyric with phases of her own life—her happy childhood when Archie Squires took her to the circus, her marriage to the most wonderful man in the world, how she cried when he left her but quickly got used to being alone. When she reaches the "I remember the day that my house caught fire," the sob in the voice is for real. And finally she reacts to the many letters she has received over the years, telling her that if she is *so* fed of life then why not just end it all? Defiantly she declares that this will never happen, but that when death finally comes, it

176

will be no big deal. She sang neither this song nor "Megan" on the stage, declaring that it would have been too much for her emotions to cope with. Preceding this are more references to her failed marriage with "The Way We Were", from the Barbara Streisand film of the same name.

The album—completed just days after Dot and Tom went their separate ways—ends with a stroke of genius. For despite all that has happened in her life, despite the trials and tribulations that he put her through at the time, and the fact that she has never *really* gotten over him no matter how many times she has tried to kid herself, Roger Moore is so foremost in her thoughts that he is now directly referred to. In "If I Had a Chance", one of the finest songs she ever wrote, Dot remembers brushing off the rice on her wedding day, his lips on hers, his promise to love her forever, and the day she watched him walk away. But she concludes that though it may be wishful thinking, if she had a chance to do it all again—to share his life and be his wife again—there would be no hesitation. Yet another Squires masterpiece!"

On 6 July 1978, Dot raised a few eyebrows when she was photographed with Marc Rowe, the light-middleweight boxing champion—thirty years her junior—who had won a gold medal at the 1966 Commonwealth Games. The occasion was the London charity premiere of *The Wild Geese*, starring Roger Moore and Richard Burton. But, I and her circle wanted to know, was he a replacement for Tom? She found this amusing.

"That's for me to know and for you and everybody else to find out," she said. "Roger certainly gave me a funny look—but the Italian kept her distance, otherwise I'd have bloody well told her that she wasn't the only one who could pull a grab a pretty guy, and that if I *had* grabbed him, then I hadn't grabbed him from somebody else!"

"Me, no slap again and showing a bit of leg!"

Dot enjoying a tipple with this author…just!

Dot, welcoming her beloved Esban into the winners'
enclosure, 1965

Surprising Helen Shapiro on her birthday

July 1978, with light-middleweight boxer Mark Rowe
at the premiere of *The Wild Geese.*

"Hats, gloves and glasses!"

12: At The End Of The Day

"What drives me is the applause. Once it's there in the bloodstream, you can't get it out. It's not the pay-cheque, it's the feeling that an audience loves you." Dorothy Squires.

On 8 December 1979, Dot opened for a week-long stint at London's 2,000-seater Dominion Theatre, in Tottenham Court Road. She did not finance the concerts herself, though she did pay for the three of the shows to be recorded. It must be said, the technicians could have done a better job. Several of her best songs were omitted from the subsequent album, her first and last on her own Esban label, whilst others were included here which might have been better left off. She recalled:

> I made an absolute hash of "Can't Smile Without You" on the night of the premiere because camera flashes were going off all over the place, and this put me off. I sang it much better in the other shows, but it was my bad performance which ended up on the LP. They also left off "I Remember It Well" and "Something Greater". But who was I to argue? I was only paying for the bloody thing! And by the way, what did you think of the LP cover?

"It was awful," I said. "Your worst since *Cheese And Wine*, though even that one wasn't as bad as the one they used for *Reflections*, with the dolly-bird on the cover!"

Dot opened each show with "A Lovely Way To Spend An Evening", but the running order of her songs differed each evening. Kris Kristofferson's "Help Me Make It Through The Night" was amended to incorporate the Welsh folk song, "All Through The Night", whilst Morris Albert's "Feelings" was embellished, to express how she is

182

missing her great love, Roger Moore once again. After "Never, Never, Never", an Italian song which had taken Mina to the top of the European charts, comes perhaps the ultimate lampooning of her ex-husband when she duets with someone she introduces as Monty on the Lerner-Loewe song from *Gigi.* Dot's lyrics are hilariously irreverent—Maurice Chevalier and Hermione Gingold she and Monty are not. She turned up late for their date the other night because she says she was with Nick—he says she was *in* the nick. "Monty, you're a bore," she sings—bringing his response, "So is Roger Moore!" sending the audience wild. She asks who this is and Monty says he played The Saint—whilst she cracks, "I've got news for you, pal. A Saint he ain't!" Then they go on to sing about how Monty walked her home one night—and she lost her virginity to him on the wet grass. Classic! Off the stage, Dot was one of the wittiest people I knew—classy even when cursing the air blue—and it is a little sad that she did not add little patters like this to more of her shows.

Suffice to say, for legal reasons, "I Remember It Well" was omitted from the LP, though it did turn up some years later on the double CD issued by President featuring highlights from these shows and those in Llanelli. Fans felt decidedly cheated over this, for there was enough material in the archives, left off the original albums, to have made up a double-CD of each. Dot next sings a reworked "We Clowns". More high-powered than the studio version, it opens with the introduction to the aria "Vesta la giubba" from *Pagliacci*, and ends with her singing the final bars of this. She "serenades" Kenny Brown with "I'm Glad There Is You", raises the roof with "You'll Never Walk Alone", and closes with a medley of her four chart hits. Her version of "My Way" here is arguably her best ever live recording of the song, which indeeed is saying something.

After the Dominion concerts, Dot was conspicuous by her absence for almost three years, certainly so far the media was concerned. An exception was a sarcastic piece in one of the tabloids asking if she was still alive. There were sell-out concerts up and down the country, and in 1982 she was the first popular entertainer to perform at London's recently inaugurated Barbican Concert Hall. Early in 1983, she began working on a new album for Pye, entitled *May You Always*, after the Joan Regan hit. Eleven songs were selected, all of which had been performed at the Dominion Theatre, and arranged by Dot and Nicky Welsh. These were about to be recorded when she was told that, "due to unforeseen circumstances", the Pye recording unit headed by Howard Barrow, who had worked on most of her later recordings, had been cancelled and the editing and mixing of the tapes assigned to someone else. She told Mike Dow of *OUT* magazine:

> We've now had to go back into the studio and put a lot of work into the recording, as it has to be up to the standard of the recordings of my Palladium concerts in 1970/71/72. We've put in extra instruments and with the help of my engineers and the latest recording techniques have updated the recording, and the result is magnificent, but it has cost me £25,000 to date. The routine includes "New York, New York" as well as "May You Always", which voices my feelings for the public. There's a specialness in my audiences as they have believed in me and their belief has helped me carry on.

Ten of the songs for *May You Always* were recorded. Dot had dropped "A Lovely Way To Spend An Evening" as this had been used as an opener for the shows and she no longer felt that it fitted in with the other material. Arrangements had been made to record two more songs—"I Am What I Am" and Don Gibson's "I'd Be A Legend In My Time", when Nicky Welsh was given the invidious task of telling her that the album had been shelved. She recalled:

184

They didn't have the guts to tell me personally, and I was never given a real reason for the LP being cancelled. So I decided there and then that I would never sign another record contract as long as I lived.

Dot was good to her word. These last two songs were recorded with her own Esban label—not in a studio, but in single takes by Howard Barrow on the stage in an empty theatre, and with the backing singers added later. Dot even donned a Douglas Darnell gown to give the occasion a "live" feel—the only time so far as I know that she sang in black. "I'd Be A Legend In My Time" is good, but would have benefited a retake as she misses her first cue. "I Am What I Am" is exceptional. Then as now the undisputed anthem of the gay community, it had been written by Jerry Herman for George Hearne to perform in the musical, *La Cage Aux Folles*. Dot also had a final dig at the studio she had accused of deserting her—for on the label she had the words printed, "Engineered at *Pie* Studios."

"But it was the truth," she said. "I mean, when we'd done we all sat in the back of the theatre and ate pies!"

"I Am What I Am" pushed Dot in a new direction, in the twilight years of her career—performing in classy gay clubs such as Rockshots, in Leeds, which she officially opened, but only as a guest. Other than four songs sung to a backing tape, there was no concert that night.

"Tonight I'm a scarlet woman," she announced, referring to her bright red Darnell gown.

Dot's penultimate studio recording was a curiosity entitled "I, The Chosen One", co-authored with Kenny Brown and put down in December 1983, though this would not be released during her lifetime.

During our chats we talked about my French singers. Dot was a Piaf fan, but had not heard of Barbara (1930-97) until I sent her some tapes. When we discussed my book, *Great Ladies of Song*, Marie Dubas (1898-1972) came up.

Marie had been a friend of Gracie Fields and her most famous song, a *chanson-parlée*, had been "La priere de la Charlotte", which tells the story of a pregnant prostitute who goes to Notre Dame to pray—and begs the Virgin Mary to let her baby die so that it might not suffer the way she has.

"She sounds a really cheerful bugger," Dot had quipped. "What did she do for an encore, work as an embalmer?"

Now she confessed to having taken a leaf out of Marie's book and written "I, The Chosen One", a maudlin, lengthy poem in which she is accompanied not by an orchestra, but by Kenny Brown on the synthesiser. One needs to know what Dot was all about to understand her ranting, otherwise one might come to the conclusion that she is under the influence. Not so! She is offering a heartfelt prayer within which she unleashes her pent-up fury over the hurt and pain she suffered since the Payola scandal. Cursing "those men who made me walk in fear", she pleads with God and tells Him:

> *Those putrid souls can never belong to you!*
> *For I will never forget those lonely, frightened years,*
> *When I hung my guiltless head in shame!*

And where the Marie Dubas song ends, "Virgin Mary, full of grace, pray for us poor sinners," Dot concludes:

> *Blessed am I, the chosen one!*

It was Dot who helped spring the surprise on her friend Jenny Pitman when she became Eamon Andrews' "victim" on *This Is Your Life* on 28 March 1984. Pitman observed how she had been driven to the Theatre Royal, Drury Lane for a photo-shoot, that as she had walked up the stairs she had heard a familiar voice, singing:

186

"Is that Dorothy Squires?" I asked. "Yes, it is," said the photographer. "She's rehearsing. Would you like to say hello?" We approached the double doors and as we stepped inside I could see Dot singing with the band in the spotlight, and then vaguely in the dimmed light I could see my solicitor, the vet and one or two other familiar faces. "Oh," I thought. "This must be a surprise party." But the next second, from behind a screen out popped Eamon Andrews. "Jenny Pitman, this is your life!" I had been led like a lamb to the slaughter. I was *caught*.

In April 1984, Dot received a call from Diana Dors' third husband, Alan Lake, informing her that Diana was in the final stages of the ovarian cancer that had ravaged her for the last two years. She headed straight for Diana's home, to learn that her friend had been admitted to the Princess Margaret Hospital for surgery to remove an internal blockage. By now the cancer had spread to her bone marrow and the doctors told Lake—who had insisted that Dot should be present when they delivered their prognosis—that there was no hope of saving her. Newsreel footage of Dot entering and leaving the hospital shows her looking very distressed. On 4 March, Diana died, aged just 52.

Five months later, unable to handle life without her—and in his grief oblivious to the fact that he had a 14-year-old son, Jason—Alan Lake shot himself, and amongst the many stories appearing in the tabloids was one proclaiming that Dot intended making Jason a ward of court. She denied this, telling *OUT*'s Mike Dow:

> They put it quite succinctly saying if it was necessary, I would go to make him a ward of court. Of course, I could not do that as I'm not a relation. My first thoughts when I heard Alan had shot himself was Jason. But I would not interfere. In a matter of weeks this will have blown over—and he'll

need friends then, won't he? I've no intention of ever interfering with that child at all. But if he ever needs friends, I'll be there.

Diana's home for the past twenty years, Orchard Manor, was sold by her lawyers, and its contents and her jewellery sold at auction. Once all the bills, outstanding tax payments and death duties had been settled, there was little left. Jason *was* made a ward of court, but to his half-brother, Gary Dawson, from their mother's second marriage.

In November that year, Dot taped three songs that I had adapted for her from the original French. "I Wear My Heart Upon My Sleeve" had started out as "Je porte ma vie", and had been a hit for my friend, Gérard Berliner (1956-2010). "The Unknown Town" had been introduced by Edith Piaf as "La ville inconnue" in her famous recital of December 1960 at the Paris Olympia. When I was singing in the clubs, I always put this one at the end of my set which often included a tribute to Dot with "For Once In My Life" and "My Way":

> *In the unknown town, people pass me by,*
> *Though they all know my name, they don't ask why*
> *I drift from street to street, it's an endless chain,*
> *Have I been here before? Will I come here again?*

The third song was "Solitude", written and performed by the previously mentioned Barbara, France's greatest singer after Piaf. Dot liked her, but initially was not keen on the song:

> *Waiting behind the door each night when I come home,*
> *Hiding in the shadows, lurking in the gloom…*
> *Reflections of the loves I've lost*
> *And chances that have passed me by,*

Those things I loved and hated most,
That made me laugh and sometimes made me cry.

"It reminds me too much of 'Solitude's My Home'," Dot said. "It's not *bad* but I think I much prefer the other two."

To date, none of these recordings have resurfaced. I will never forget the day when I presented Dot with the first one. I will not name the venue—save that the lady in question was the Lady Mayor, and my wife was asked to take a few photographs of their meeting in Dot's dressing-room.

"I feel just like a racehorse," said the Lady Mayor, with an air of grandeur.

"You fucking look like one," I heard Dot mutter under her breath, as did the Lady Mayor.

That same evening, a journalist strode up to Dot and asked how her "daughter" Rosemary was doing. He was referring to the singer Rosemary Squires, born in 1928.

"Don't talk wet man," she shot back, though she was only joking. "She's probably old enough to be MY mother!"

By now, Dot's addiction to litigation had begun taking over her career. To date there had been 33 court cases, few of which she had won. On 1 October 1986, having spent so much on these, she was declared bankrupt at Slough County Court. Soon afterwards Sir Michael Havers, the Attorney-General, declared her a vexatious litigant which prohibited her from launching any further lawsuits without first obtaining permission from the High Court.

Dot had a particular beef with Havers, a friend of Kenneth More who had advised him how to tackle her when she had sued him in the wake of the 1968 BAFTA awards ceremony.

"The swine never liked me," she said. "It's taken him nigh on twenty years to get even. Another one who's hand-in-glove with the establishment."

Evicted from her Bray home, her possessions were seized and sold off at a public auction in Reading to pay off

189

her debts. For several weeks she lived at a bed-and-breakfast until a fan, Doris Joyce, kindly came to her rescue and allowed her to rent—at a nominal cost—her cottage in Ackworth, West Yorkshire. We lived just five miles away at the time. The woman who at the height of her career had been worth an estimated £2 million was now reduced to living on record and song-writing royalties. She confessed to having around £30,000 in a bank account "for a rainy day", but swore never to touch it. So far as is known, she never did. She confessed in her final televised interview:

> I have gone through half a million in counsels and lawyers' fees. When the *News of the World* published 'When Love Turned Sour', that was the beginning of the end for me because of the vendetta I was subjected to after that. And I hold Rupert Murdoch entirely responsible for it.

Even so, this indomitable champion refused to give in. She still talked about producing *Old Rowley*, planned more concert tours, a return to the Palladium—even a recital at the Paris Olympia which still would not have been possible, even had she wanted to hire the hall herself. Bruno Coquatrix had died, but her name was still on a French theatres blacklist. The Palladium *might* have worked, and the Liverpool Empire and Birmingham Hippodrome *were* interested for a little while until she began making extraneous demands.

Dot's studio swansong was on 14 January 1987. "The Wine Is There", self-composed and released as a single on her Esban label with "Try A Little Tenderness" on the flipside. The former was ruined in that it was a duet with a raucous vocalist named on the label as Darren Wells. It starts off well enough with Dot coming in after a harmonica solo, inspired by listening to one of my singers—Piaf had used such an intro for "La ville inconnue", as did Dot on the tape-recording of my English adaptation. She reflects on the love she lost for the very last time, saying that they were so in love that words were never necessary, and concludes that, should he wish to pick up where they left off, the wine will be there, ready to be poured. Wells enters the proceedings at this point to muck everything up, much of the time singing woefully out of tune. Otherwise her faithful team were all there to salvage a little of this otherwise great song: Kenny Brown on piano, Johnnie Gray on sax, Mac Swann on drums, under the baton of Nicky Welsh, who sadly died the following year.

Dot had the flu when she sang at the Astoria Ballroom in Leeds in 1988. Accompanied on the synthesiser by Kenny Brown she was on stage for just over an hour, shorter than her usual concert, and forgot the words to "My Way". The fans went wild just the same. On 17 March 1990, she sang for the last time at Brighton's Dome Theatre. She had been booked by Brian Ralphe, of The Glitterbugs drag-act, a man she admired because he had fought in the Falklands War and been decorated for bravery. The voice had by now lost some of its power, but her arrangements had been toned down to accommodate this and the press reported that she had given an exemplary performance.

What would be Dot's last major review was penned posthumously by "Pariss", a journalist with the gay magazine, QX, and who as a child had lived near Dot in Bexley. Recalling her spats with the local police and tradesmen he ungallently observed, "She was a belter of a singer in the Ethel Merman mould, but not someone you wanted to live next to, or even in the same village." His review of Dot's performance was a mixture of sarcasm and over-the-top enthusiasm, though he came right in the end:

> The legend I saw on stage that night lived up to the caricature portrayed by a hundred drag queens of the 70s and 80s. A tiny figure swathed in organza—

clutching a flower, belting out numbers that filled every corner of the theatre. Never mind that she forgot most of the words except the chorus. Never mind that she swayed drunkedly about the stage and never mind that her language would have made a docker blush. Her star quality oozed across the footlights like Judy and Marilyn before her, for it was her very fallibility that endeared her to her legions of loyal fans across the years. In this, her last ever performance (although we didn't know it) she, as ever, gave her all. Well, all that there was to give.

Soon after hanging up her Douglas Darnell gowns for the last time, Dot offered legal advice of a kind to Dusty Springfield, after the singer—who had once borrowed one of her costumes for a concert—saw red when the comedian Bobby Davro lampooned her in a sketch on his television show. Like Dot, Dusty was used to being emulated by drag acts but found the image of Davro—wearing high heels and a cheap wig, swigging from a bottle and staggering across the stage whilst slurring the words to "What Have I Done To Deserve This?"—*too* unsettling.

She may not however have taken the matter further had it not been for Dot, who recalled, "I told her, 'Sue the hell out of them, Dusty. Once you let these bastards get away with robbing you of your dignity, they just keep on doing it. Take some advice from one who knows!'"

Oddly, it was not Davro that Dusty sued, but the television company. She had *had* a drink problem, she confessed, but for eight years now not one drop of alcohol had passed her lips. The court awarded her £75,000 in damages, and ordered ITV to make a public apology.

In the autumn of 1994, following Doris Joyce's death the year before, Dot was served with an eviction order to leave the cottage in Ackworth. According to Ross Benson, writing in the *Daily Express*, she contacted Roger Moore and asked him to fork out the £60,000 to buy the property. Dot virulently denied this:

> Absolute bollocks made up by that fucking gossip columnist with his airs and graces and fancy suits. Then there's the other one who tells everyone he's a close friend of everybody, when he doesn't know them from Adam. You know the one I'm talking about, the one who's been pestering me. In all my life I have *never* asked for hand-outs. Apologies to you and those lovely people up in Yorkshire, darling, but I never really wanted to *live* up here. That's why I'm going home to Wales.

The "other one", still alive at the time of writing and thus unable to be named, had been given the nickname "The Grim Reaper" by my friend the singer Elizabeth Welch, because he prayed on stars who were about to die, then after their demise proclaimed he had been a close friend and confidant, when there was no one else around to prove otherwise. Another journalist disliked by Dot—though in truth there were hardly any that she *did* like or trust—was Quentin Letts, who upset her by writing in his *Daily Telegraph* Peterborough column:

> In three weeks Dorothy Squires will be homeless. She had some money recently but gave it to a horse sanctuary....She was once a great name in show business with a string of racehorses. When Mrs. Joyce died in 1993 Miss Squires faced the loss of her place, and sympathetic donations from fans arrived in numbers....."But I could not spend their money," says Miss Squires. Instead she gave it to a local equine sanctuary, in memory of the steeds she once owned.

"That's absolute rubbish," Dot exclaimed, after I called and

193

read this out to her. "I never spoke to that reporter. Some fans sent me money, it's true, but I sent it back to them and said *they'd* be better off giving it to a horse sanctuary. I didn't give their money away!"

"And what about your family, Dot?" I asked her. "Is there none of them that can help you out?"

The receiver certainly rattled as she responded to this one:

> My *relatives*? Holy fuck, I guess if the shoe was on the other foot, mine would be the first door they'd come knocking on. Most of the time, the only time my relatives have wanted me is when they've wanted something for themselves. I haven't had anything to do with any of them for the past six years, and I've no intention of doing so now. They've tried to call me here [in Ackworth] but each time they do, instead of telling them to get lost, I just put the phone down.

Dot was the subject of the *Daily Mail*'s *Saturday Profile*, a largely unflattering and error-riddled retrospective of her career penned by Jessica Davies, and who ungallantly opined in her introduction to the piece:

> The tale of Dorothy Squires is a desperately sad one, inviting comparisons with Norma Desmond, the faded and deluded silent-movie star in *Sunset Boulevard*. For Dorothy Squires, too, was once a star—a pint-sized glamourpuss from South Wales, draped in lush furs and feather boas, a woman whose popular Fifties recordings brought her wealth, and marriage to a handsome younger man...Today she is a lonely, impoverished old woman a few months off her 80th birthday, who could soon be made homeless from the modest Yorkshire cottage where she lives as a recluse.

194

Davies quoted Dot as having said of her reluctance to grant Roger Moore a divorce, "I made up my mind that the woman who possessed him would at least never become his wife." She also mentioned a quip made on-stage by Dot at the Dominion Theatre, when she had joked that her life story was about to be turned into a film—with Barbra Streisand playing her!

"It was a joke, for Christ's sake," Dot exclaimed. "Bloody hell, is the woman *so* stupid as to *believe* that?"

Davies had tracked down Robin McGibbon of Everest Books, the would-be publisher of *Rain, Rain Go Away* who allegedly rued the day he had met Dot on account of her insistence that Roger Moore's love-letters should be included in her book. McGibbon's wife, Sue, recalled Dot taking her into her bedroom in Bexley to show her the collection of furs and sequinned dresses, and a safe filled with jewellery. According to Mrs. McGibbon, Dot told her:

> I promise you, you can have all of this if [Roger] sues. But those letters must go in. Because one day it will be raining, and there will be thunder and lightning and the wind will be howling and I will hear a knock at the door. And he'll be standing there, drenched, begging me and saying, "You know I loved you, Dorothy." And then I'll slam the door.

Dot returned to Wales, to Trebanog in the Rhondda Valley, to live in a house owned by another fan, Esme Coles. The move coincided with a poignant piece penned by Patrick Newley in *The Stage And Television Today*, which made her cry. Headed "Dorothy Come Home", Newley posed:

> Whatever happened to Dorothy Squires? One of this country's most successful performers on stage and record, little is heard of this showbiz legend these days. Dorothy Squires was and always will be something of an enigma. To the outsider and the

uninitiated, the adulation and adoration heaped upon her may seem curious....Wild, frenzied ovations used to greet her entrances on stage, There was applause at the beginning of her songs which she did not even originally record....She is perhaps the only singer of her time in this country who actually embodies her own songs—a total belief in each number, which in its own individual way becomes something of a tragic or comic autobiography. In this respect she is closest to Judy Garland (who Squires holds rightly and respectfully in near idolatry)....Her personality and offstage antics have frequently overshadowed her own talent. Who can forget her thumping a startled Adrienne Corri over the head on live television, when Miss Corri insulted the memory of Garland? Who can forget the showbiz jokes about her having a travel pass to the High Courts in London for libel cases? As always the lady has style....In a unique and idiosyncratic show business career Squires is at the top of her own hill, always making headlines, her own "cock-eyed optimist and as such in the end it is the artist and the stylist who has the last laugh. The songs go on and the style of Squires remains beautifully intact.

Doris Joyce had latterly insisted that Dot live *rent-free* in her cottage, but all this had changed with her death. There had however been no written agreement. Dot explained:

There didn't need to be. We were friends, and there was no need to write everything down. And poor Doris was not even in her grave before they began sending people around, hammering on the door. So I left the avaricious buggers in the lurch.

On 12 May 1995, Dot was served with a final eviction order

and given 21 days to vacate a property which she had already left. The much-despised Ross Benson reported under the headline, "Squires Gypsy Life Turns Full Circle":

> Joan Chambers, sister of the late owner of the cottage, says: "She has not paid a penny rent. All we have received is a very small sum towards repairs. There was no option but to apply for a court order. She talks incessantly about all the money she expects to win back from her trustees in bankruptcy and legal cases she lost. She also says that she has jewellery and investments in London. If so, why not sell them and buy a home of her own?

Benson sarcastically concluded:

> So the Squires caravan rolls on...back to Wales. For the star, whose first hit record was The Gypsy, the turbulent life that began in the back of a travelling van parked in a Welsh field, has come full circle.

It could be argued that, even if Dot *was* living in the cottage rent-free, it should have been the owners' responsibility to pay for any repairs. Benson was being unspeakably heartless with his closing comment, and its suggestion that Dot had returned to living in a field.

Early in 1996, Dot fell ill and was diagnosed with a tumour on her bladder. She was told that this *was* operable, and as a matter of course and still wanting nothing to do with her relatives, she named Roger Moore as her next of kin. It was he who, without being asked, paid for her surgery and stay in a private hospital. The surgeon who conducted the operation made an alarming discovery—Dot, who had hardly ever smoked and nagged at her friends, including myself, to "give up the weed"—had lung cancer, too far advanced to effect a cure. Given but a

197

short time to live, she kept the news to herself. The *only* ones aware of how really ill she was were Esme Coles and Roger Moore.

She told Anne de Courcy, of Moore's generosity, "I don't like the things he's done but I have very warm feelings for the man himself."

At the end of 1997—shortly after I called her to tell her that my friend Barbara had died in Paris, though we spent much of the time talking about Princess Diana, who had died in August—Dot gave her first television interview in years, for BBC Wales, and which sadly turned out to be her last.

Rain, Rain Go Away: The Dorothy Squires Story, was directed by David Howard, narrated by one-off *James Bond* actor George Lazenby and complemented with those of her songs, played in the background, that applied mostly to her personal life: "We Clowns", "If I Never Sing Another Song", "Is That All There Is?"

Standing behind the counter of her shop, Esme Coles tells of how a friend read in a local newspaper that Dot was being evicted from her home, and how she at once got in touch, to find Dot pretending to be her secretary when she answered the phone, something she often did—with me, as I knew and spoke to her secretaries, she pretended to be her sister until assured that it really was me on the line. Even when offered a house to live in, rent free, she was what might be described as "charismatically demanding"—more to do with being afraid of being seen than being difficult, when telling Esme that she would be there the next morning, at a-quarter-to-six, and then turning up with cases filled mostly with documents.

"It was like my mother had come home," Esme recalled.

In her last television interview, Dot added a little more to the Billy Reid story and her ending of their relationship, saying that the last straw had come one evening when she had been held up in the wings, because the zipper on her dress had stuck. Whilst her sister Renee had been helping her with the problem, Reid had gestured to the packed house that Dot was late because she was drunk. She also reflects upon the pain of being compelled to move home:

> I have moved nine times, in lorries—my personal clothes, everything….I was in this one room for about two months. I'd lost everything. My house I paid cash for, my eight horses, my personal wardrobe, everything. I was out in the street with just one case. Now you just imagine, I'm like a bloody beggar.

She shows the cameraman the four fur coats that she salvaged, and exclaims, "These, I had to thieve out of my own house, at night."

She almost turns on her unseen interviewer when asked the unscripted question about her enforced solitude, a trait she had in common towards the end of her life with another of my close friends, Marlene Dietrich, who had told me the same thing many times:

> When you've been accused of so much, you can't go out and face the world because they only believe what they read. Don't you *understand*? All right, so I'll ask *you* the question. If it had happened to you, how would *you* feel? I have great pride. I've had thousands follow me. How can I go out with everything bad that's been written about me? You tell me how *you* would face people? What do you think it's like when I put my head on a pillow at night?

The day before the BBC Wales interview was scheduled to be broadcast, Dot collapsed in her living-room. Esme Coles found her and summoned a doctor, and he subsequently admitted her to the Llwynypia Hospital, Mid Glamorgan.

199

Esme Coles told *The Times*, "She loved Roger Moore until the very end. He was the only man for her. I was so concerned over Dorothy's health, I contacted Roger. He rang the hospital to give Dorothy his best wishes, and has kept in touch every day since."

By now, Dot's niece, Emily, had arrived on the scene and according to her, Roger Moore rang the hospital and told her, "Take hold of her hand, give it a little squeeze and tell her Roger is thinking of her."

According to Emily, Dot smiled and said, "Magic."

And it was in the early hours of Tuesday 14 April 1998 that Dorothy Squires, arguably Britain's greatest female singer of the twentieth century, slipped away, leaving her adoring fans and friends bereft.

A few years earlier, I had asked her what she would like her epitaph to be, and she had sung down the phone:

> *If within your heart there's love,*
> *That's a blessing from above,*
> *With these things you've got a lot,*
> *Look around, look what you've got…*

Epilogue

It was a bad year for celebrity deaths: Frank Sinatra, with whom she had shared "My Way", died exactly one month after Dot. Other losses in 1998 included tennis champion Helen Wills Moody, broadcaster Frank Muir, Enoch Powell, actor Daniel Massey (on Dot's birthday), bandleader Syd singer Tammy Wynette, Linda McCartney, and novelist Catherine Cookson.

In death, Dot proved no less controversial than in life. As often happens with estranged families of celebrities, arguments were reported over the funeral arrangements. According to a hospital spokesman, when Dot's niece arrived in Trebanog, Dot had already lapsed into the coma from which she would not emerge. If this is true, then it is unlikely that she heard Roger Moore's final message, and equally unlikely that she pronounced the word, "Magic!"

Dot had told me many times that she had wanted nothing to do with her family, and that this had been the case for many years. I assume she told other friends the same. What is sad is that the person who helped her most in her last years—Esme Coles—did not attend her funeral on account of the alleged animosity levelled towards her, and which was not helped by interfering journalists. It is equally understandable that Esme refused to allow Emily Squires access to Dot's home which of course belonged not to Dot, but to Esme.

On the eve of the funeral, the press reported Emily as having offered Esme "an olive branch" though Dot's friends will always argue it should have been the other way round, as it was Esme who had taken Dot in when she had been at her lowest ebb, and cared for her until the end. William Hickey reported in the *Daily Express*:

> This follows, as I disclosed, Esme's refusal to let Emily Jane enter Dorothy's Trebanog home on Thursday, after which the police were called. Emily

Jane tells me, "I did not see my aunt for seven years until I came to her in hospital, but we spoke on the phone regularly. I am hugely grateful to Esme for what she did for my aunt. I have asked how many seats she wants for the funeral but she has said no. If there is a rift, it is not on my side."

What I and many others found not just curious, but offensive and profoundly hurtful, was "The Squires Family" decision, which I was made aware of by way of a letter signed by their spokesman, "Desmond Mainwaring Brown", to return the "Get Well" and "With Sympathy" cards sent to the hospital by Dot's closest friends. Brown, who cites himself as Dot's lifelong friend, but who none of us had heard of until the letters dated 10 June were sent out from Port Talbot, declared in his handwritten missive, which for legal reasons I have paraphrased:

> Shortly before Dot's death, they [one presumes he means the family] discussed answering the multitude of cards that she had received from people and friends with get well wishes. They therefore agreed that he [Brown] would answer them on her behalf. He adds that at this particular time, they had been unaware that Dot had cancer, and that unfortunately she never recovered, and that she died on 14 April soon after her birthday—unaware that she had the disease, the news of which they kept from her. Sadly, Brown concludes, Dot is gone but she has left behind a legacy of songs which will never be replaced, performed with a voice which was a gift to only one person in the whole wide world. Finally he writes that he has included the hymn sheet and the order of service for the funeral—two months too late.

Again, according to the hospital spokesman, the *only* ones who had known the exact nature of Dot's illness were Esme Coles, and Roger Moore.

On 21 April, in dreadful weather conditions, a service was held at St Mary's Church, Port Talbot. The hymns were "Oh Lord my God, When I in Awesome Wonder" and "The Day Thou Gavest Lord Is Ended", chosen by Dot herself. Olwyn Rees whose husband Johnny Tudor had sometimes worked as Dot's support act—most famously at the Palladium in 1970—recited a poem, "All Is Well", whilst Welsh actor Sion Probert recited Dylan Thomas' "And Death Shall Know No Dominion".

Three days later, a second service took place at Streatham Park Cemetery. Dorothy's coffin was brought into the chapel whilst her recording of "Song of the Valley" was broadcast over loud-speakers. Russ Conway played "Say It With Flowers, after which he and Norman Newell led the mourners into a chorus of "My Thanks To You", written by Newell for Steve Conway, one of Dot's favourite singers who died in 1952, aged 31. Her coffin was carried out to the strains of "My Way", to loud applause from the crowd outside. She was buried with her brother, Freddie. There were floral tributes from around the world. Danny La Rue, still not welcomed back into the fold, opted not to show his face but sent a wreath, as did Douglas Darnell, Shirley Bassey, and Dusty Springfield—now in the latter stages of cancer to which she would succumb the following year. The one which would have mattered most to her was the bouquet of purple tulips from Roger Moore inscribed, "I've said it with flowers!" She sleeps in good company. Nearby are the graves of bandleader Charlie Kunz, comedians Will Hay and Ben Warris, actor Wilfred Brambell, "Lambeth Walk" composer Lupino Lane, and music-hall star Florrie Forde.

The *Guardian* eulogised her "a show business monster in an age of reasonable pygmies". *The Times* called her, "Sentimental, tender and intensely dramatic, a sort of Bette

203

Davis of song elegising the pain of lost love and the timorous hope of learning to love again."

The last word, however, should be left to her friend Patrick Newley, who observed in *The Stage*:

> Over the years, I got to know Squires well. She was indeed a difficult woman and her personality and off-stage antics frequently overshadowed her own talent. But at the height of her fame no one was more talked about in theatrical circles, mimicked on stage by lesser performers, and worshipped off stage by the curious and the faithful. Yet lines that she said on stage such as "Can I be blamed for trying too hard?", "It's been a lonely climb", and "I may never make it and maybe I will", stick in the memory. In a unique and idiosyncratic career Squires was always top of her own hill, always making headlines, and in the end it is the artist and the stylist who have the last laugh. The songs go on and the style of Squires remains beautifully intact.

Appendix I
Dorothy Squires Discography

The following represents Dorothy Squires' complete UK and international shellac and vinyl catalogue *so far as is known*. Note: the names of the composers and lyricists are only included the first time the song is listed. ND = No other details such as composers, etc. Unreleased records and tape recordings are included when the song has not otherwise been commercially released.

1937
Decca F6224 When The Poppies Bloom Again (Pelosi/Towers/Morrow) Rec 12/36 ND

Regal Zonophone
MR2522   Sweet Heartache (Washington/Stept)
            Moon At Sea (Pease/Rose/Stock)*
            *duet with Ivor Davies

Regal Zonophone
MR2523   Kiss Me Goodnight (Spoliansky)
            You Needn't Have Kept A Secret (ND)

Regal Zonophone
MR2607   Moonlight On The Waterfall (Kennedy)
            The First Time I Saw You (ND)

Regal Zonophone
MR2638   Whistling Gypsy Waltz (Damerell/Evans)
            My Gypsy Dream Girl (Pease/Harvey)

1938
Regal Zonophone
MR2663   So Many Memories (Woods) Rec 12/37
            Don't Forget The Old Folks (vocal Ivor Davies) ND.

Regal Zonophone
MR2664   *6-Hit Medley*: Side 1: The First Time I Saw
              You/ Blossoms On Broadway/Remember
              Me (Dubin/ Shrilket/Rainger/Warren)
              Side 2: Old Pal Of Mine/Little Old Lady/
              Afraid To Dream* Rec 12/37 *Side Two not
              by Dorothy.

Regal Zonophone
MR2690   Little Drummer Boy (Pelosi/Noel)
              Remember Me

Regal Zonophone
MR2691   Are You Sincere (Grunland)
              The Sweetest Thing in The World (ND)*
              *Not performed by Dorothy

Regal Zonophone
MR2783   Rose Covered Shack (Durono/Noel)
              The Chocolate Soldier's Daughter
              (Kennedy/Carr)

Regal Zonophone
MR2784   The Sweetest Sweetheart Of All (Messini/
              Parr-Davies)
              My Heaven In The Pines (Conrad)

1945
Parlophone F2076 Coming Home (Reid)
              Dreams of Yesterday (Heatherton)

Parlophone F2080 Waiting (Ravazza/Milton/Lawrence)
              Just A Prayer Away (Kapp/Tobias)

Parlophone F2085 The Gypsy (Reid)
              Safe in My Arms Again (Reid)

Parlophone F2101 Under The Willow Tree (Reid)
Goodnight Until Tomorrow (Evan/Foster)

Parlophone F2102 I'll Close My Eyes (Reid)
Let The Rest Of The World Go By
(Brennan/Ball)

Parlophone F2218 Curly Top (Reid)
Yippee Ally Ay Ho (Reid)

1946
Parlophone F2137 Sweet Dreams To You
(Bradley/Douglas)
Memories Of You (Razaf/Blake)

Parlophone F2146 I'd Like To Get You Alone (Prichard)
It's A Pity To Say Goodnight (Reid)

Parlophone F2165 Save A Piece Of Wedding Cake (Reid)
Laughing On The Outside, Crying On The
Inside (Raleigh/Wayne)

Parlophone F2175 There's A Fairy In My Garden (Reid)
Old Friends Are Golden Friends (Gilbert)

Parlophone F2182 Three Beautiful Words Of Love (Reid)
My Man Didn't Come Back (Reid)

Parlophone F2196 I Love You For Sentimental Reasons
(Watson/ Best)
I Get Along With Somebody Else (Reid)

Parlophone F2208 When China Boy Meets China Girl
(Reid)
The Old Apple Tree Will Bloom Again
(Strauss/Miller/Denby/Watson)

Parlophone F2225 Unchangeable You (Reid)
　　　　　All Over Again (Watson/Denby/Barracini)

Parlophone F2244 My First Love, My Last Love, For
　　　　　Always (Reid)
　　　　　Danger Ahead, Beware (Reid)

Parlophone F2257 I'm Gonna Hold You In My Arms (Reid)
　　　　　I'm In The Mood For Love (McHugh/Fields)

1948
Parlophone F3092 A Tree In The Meadow (Reid)
　　　　　Kiss Me Once, Kiss Me More (Reid)

Columbia DB2418 After All (Reid)
　　　　　Reflections On The Water (Reid)

Columbia DB2425 Tell Me A Story (Siegler/Stock)
　　　　　Lonesome Lane (Lane)

Columbia DB2439 Break My Heart Say You Love Me
　　　　　(Reid)
　　　　　Anything I Dream Is Possible (Reid)

Columbia DB2455 Mother's Day (Reid)
　　　　　So Tired (Morgan/Stuart)

1949
Columbia DB2499 It's Spring Down Lovers Lane (Reid)
　　　　　Here Comes Me (Reid)

Columbia DB2516 If You Were Here (Greene)
　　　　　I'd Give The World To You (Peters/Carter)

Columbia DB2537 In All The World (Reid)
　　　　　Maybe Someday (Reid)

Columbia DB2573 Our Love Story (Newell/Harrison)
Too Whit, Too Whoo (Reid)

Columbia DB2605 Snowy White Snow & Jingle Bells
(Reid)
Say Goodnight But Not Goodbye (Lilly/
Moore/Cassen)

Columbia DB2610 You Shouldn't Have Kissed Me
(Gordon/Littman/Muston
We All Have A Song In Our Hearts (Yale)

1950
Columbia DB2659 Do I Worry? (Cowan/Worth)
On The Sunny Side Of The Street
(McHugh/Fields)

Columbia DB2691 Half Way To Heaven (Reid)
Just A Gramophone Record (Worth)

Columbia DB2766 Once In A While (Green/Edwards)
Baby Come Home (Louis/Muston)

ColumbiaDB2722 I Remember The Cornfields (Mayne/
Ralton)
Yes, I'll Be Here (Reid)

Odeon CE12062   I'm In The Mood For Love
Wilhemina *
*By Larry Macari & The Dutch Serenaders
(Turkish release)

Columbia DB2855 Be My Love (Cahn, Brodszky)
Life's Desire (Hargreaves/Damerell/Evans)

1951
Columbia DB2897 My Resistance Is Low (Carmichael/
Adamson)
I'll Never Know Why (Gallop/Conn)

Columbia DB2950 At The End Of The Day (O'Keefe)
And So To Sleep Again (Marsala/Skylar)

Columbia DB3005 The Little White Cloud That Cried (Ray)
Mistakes (Leslie/Lynton)

1952
Columbia DB3402 Any Time (Lawson)
I Don't Care (Drake)

Columbia DB3046 The Old Soft Shoe (Hamilton/Lewis) *
Unforgettable (Gordon) *With G H Elliott

Columbia DB3086 To Be Worthy Of You (Klages/Gross)
Be Anything But Mine (Gordis)

Columbia DB3163 Faith (Damerell/Evans)
Snowflakes (Kurtz)

1953
Columbia DB3231 Legend Of The Well (Unknown)
Maid Of The Valley (Squires)

Polygon P1068 I'm Walking Behind You (Reid)
Is There Any Room In Your Heart? (Reid)

Polygon P1076 From Your Lips To The Ears Of God
(Willmott)
Sorrento And You (Rowne)

London 451371 From Your Lips To The Ears Of God
Sorrento And You (US release)

Polygon P1077 If You Love Me (Piaf/Monnot/Parsons)
Things Go Wrong (Harrison/Turner/Esaul)

Polygon P1079 It's The Talk Of The Town (Levinson/
Neiburg/Symes)
Lost And Found (ND)

1954
Polygon P1096 Romany Violin (Tibsen/Powell)
Changing Partners (Darion/Coleman)

1955
Polygon P1149 With All My Heart (Lee aka Squires) *
White Wings (Lee aka Squires) *

Polygon P1162 When I Grow Too Old To Dream
(Romberg/Hammerstein) *
Blue, Blue, Blue (Lynne/Lee aka Squires) *
*both 78rpms with The Radio Revellers

Decca F10303 Eventide (Squires/Dunstall)
Set Me Free (Squires/Dunstall)

London 45-1465 Eventide/ Set Me Free (US release)

London 1490 Coquette (Dunstall/More aka Squires)
Precious Love (Dunstall/More aka Squires)

211

Pye Nixa N15010 When You Lose The One You Love
(Pelosi/Arden/Harper)
In All The World (Reid)

Pye Nixa N15045 I Saw The Look In Your Eyes (Astley) *
Without You (Astley/Elms/Harvey) *With Bonar Colleano

Pye Nixa N15052 What Is The Reason? (Moore aka
Squires)
Dear To Me (Moore aka Squires)

1956
Pye Nixa N15075 Come Home To My Arms (Baguley/Jane
aka Squires)
Someone To Love (Lemarque/Curtis)

Pye Nixa N15082 Precious Love (Moore aka Squires)
Banana Boat Song (Burgie/Attaway)

1957
Pye Nixa N15154 Torremolinos (Claros aka Squires)
Mother's Day

Pye Nixa N15199 Don't Search For Love (Squires)
Sticks And Stones (Squires)

Pye Nixa NEP2403 (EP) **Songs From Stars In Your Eyes**
I Saw The Look In Your Eyes;* Without You; With All My
Heart; Come Home To My Arms (not in the film).
          *With Bonar Colleano.

Columbia DB3985 Our Song (Squires)
          Song Of The Valley (Stanford)

Columbia   ??? Ivanhoe Of England
(Squires/Moore)
          Soundtrack for the TV series. Unreleased.

Vogue PNV24009 (French EP) **Someone To Love**
Someone To Love (Seule un homme peut faire ca);
Precious Love; Come Home To My Arms; The Banana
Boat Song.

1958

Pye GGL0107 (LP) *Dorothy Squires Sings Billy Reid*
Opening; It's A Pity To Say Goodnight; In All The World; I'll
Close My Eyes; Safe In My Arms; Danger Ahead; Mother's
Day; Coming Home; A Tree In The Meadow; Yes I'll Be
Here; I'm Walking Behind You; The Gypsy; Reflections On
The Water; I Still Believe.

Columbia DB4070 Bewitched (Rodgers/Hart)
        A Secret That's Never Been Told (Squires/
        Dunstall)

Decca F11262 This Place Called Home (Moore aka
        Squires)
        Trust In Me (Wever/Schwartz/Ager)

1961

Columbia DB4665 Say It With Flowers (Squires) *
        Roses Of Picardy (Wood/Weatherly) *
        *With Russ Conway

1962

Columbia DB4775 Blue Snowfall (Coleman)
        Talk It Over With Someone (Sharfenberger/
        Pinelli/Newell) With Russ Conway

Columbia DB4941 Whoever (Squires)
        How Deep Is The Ocean? (Berlin)

Columbia DB4942 Moonlight And Roses
        (Moret/Black/Lemare)
        Are You? (Squires)

1963

Columbia DB7009 Bless Your Heart My Darling (Alstone/
        Kennedy)
        Once Upon A Time (Squires)

Columbia DB7104 I Won't Cry Anymore (Squires/Dunstall)
        Red The Rose (Squires)

1964

Columbia DB7243 Look Around (Squires/Dunstall)
        Two Strangers Met (Squires)

1965

        Where In The World (Dunstall)
        Tape recording.

1966

Columbia DB7872 Someone Other Than Me (Squires/
        Dunstall)
        The Call Of Spring (Squires/Dunstall)

Decca F12159 Have I Waited Too Long (Squires/Dunstall)
        Goodbye (Squires/Dunstall)

Decca   Forevermore (Lubin/Vann) unreleased

1967

Ace of Clubs SCLR1230 LP *This Is My Life: Dorothy Squires At The Regal Cinema, Llanelli*
On A Wonderful Day Like Today (Bricusse/ Newley); Rock-A-Bye Your Baby With A Dixie Melody (Schwartz/ Lewis/Young); Mother's Day; The Gypsy; Safe In My Arms Again; I'll Close My Eyes; I'm Walking Behind You; A Lot Of Livin' To Do (Strouse/Adams); Happy Feet (Ager/ Yellen); A Tree In The Meadow; San Francisco (Kahn/ Kaper/Jurmann/Skinner); I Left My Heart In San Francisco (Cross/Cory); Tammy, Tell Me True (Squires); Shakin' The Blues Away (Berlin); When You Lose The One You Love; Yesterday (Lennon/McCartney); Everything's Coming Up Roses (Styne/Sondheim); The Song of The Valley; We'll Keep A Welcome (Jones/Joshua/Harper); Back In Your Own Back Yard (Jolson/Dreyer/Rose).

1968
President PT188 When There's Love In Your Heart
(Squires)
Where Can I Go? (Squires)

President PT213 Point Of No Return (Squires)
Roses Of Picardy (solo version)

President PT237 Your Flowers Arrived Too Late (Squires)
Red The Rose (Squires)

President PTL1023 LP   *Say It With Flowers*
Say It With Flowers; I'll Be With You In Apple Blossom
Time (Von Tilzer/Fleeson); We'll Gather Lilacs (Novello);
Moonlight And Roses; Honeysuckle Rose (Waller/Razaf);
Roses Of Picardy; Your Flowers Arrived Too Late; Tulips
From Amsterdam (Arnie/Martin);When The Poppies Bloom
Again; I'm Looking Over A Four-Leafed Clover (Woods/
Dixon); Red The Rose; Our Garden; Say It With Flowers.

Marble Arch MALS 1211 LP   *Reflections* (compilation)
It's A Pity To Say Goodnight; In All The World; I'll Close My
Eyes; Safe In My Arms; Danger Ahead; Mother's Day; A
Tree In The Meadow; Yes I'll Be Here; I'm Walking Behind
You; The Gypsy; Reflections On The Water; Coming Home

1969
President PT267 For Once In My Life Murden/Miller)
            Our Garden (Squires)

President PT281 Till (Danvers/Sigman)
            The Seasons Of (Squires)

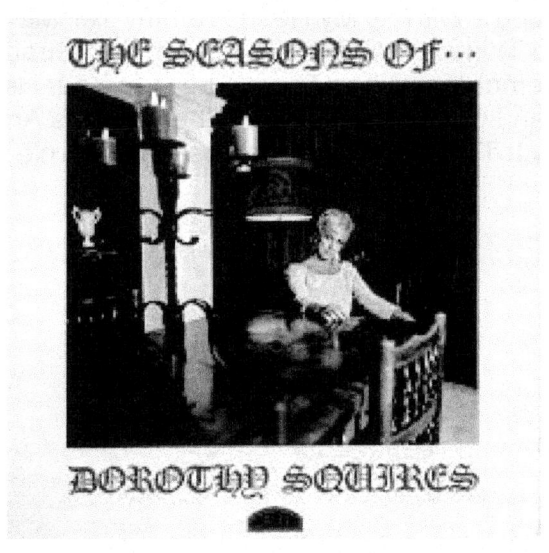

President PT1032 LP **The Seasons of Dorothy Squires**
The Seasons Of; Just In Time (Styne/Comden/Green); For
Once In My Life; Summer Place(Steiner/Discant); Kiss Me
Again (Herbert/Blossom); Till; Autumn Leaves (Kosma/
Prévert/Mercer); Who Can I Turn To (Bricusse/Newley);
Point Of No Return; Where Can I Go; I Wish You Love
(Trenet/Parsons/Turner); I Won't Cry Anymore.

President 14550AT Till/The Seasons Of (German release)

1970
JOYS 172 LP **Dorothy Sings Squires**
Look Around*; With All My Heart; Tammy Tell Me True;
The Good Things*; Point Of No Return; Two Strangers
Met; Torremolinos; When There's Love In Your Heart*;
Where Can I Go; Precious Love*;Your Flowers Arrived Too
Late; Play It To The Rules. *composed with Ernie Dunstall.

President PT305 My Way (Francois/Revaux/Thibault/Anka)
   With All My Heart

1971

President PT330 If You Love Me, Really Love Me
   Play It To The Rules (Squires)

President PT331 Where Do I Begin (Lai/Sigman)
   Look Around (Squires)

President PT337 I've Gotta Be Me (Marks)
   I Can Live Again (Squires)

President PT349 Life Goes On (Anka)
   It Can't Be Done (Squires)

President PT366 Maman (Thomas/Charnin)
   Don't Ask Me Why (Squires/Eden)

President PTLS1043/4 Double LP *Dorothy Squires At The London Palladium: Sunday December 6th 1970*
Everything Is Beautiful (Stevens); Do I Worry; *River Medley*: Way Down Upon The Swanee River (Caesar/ Gershwin)/Old Man River (Kern/Hammerstein)/Up A Lazy River (Carmichael/ (Arodin); For Once In My Life; *Autograph Book*: Why Did I Choose You (Leonard/ Martin)/If You Love Me/The Man That Got Away (Arlen/ Gershwin)/My Way/Till; *Wonderful Medley*: 'S Wonderful (Gershwin/Gershwin)/They Say It's Wonderful (Berlin)/ Wonderful One Whiteman/Grofé/Neilan/Terris); Don't Take Your Love From Me (Nemo); It's The Talk Of The Town; It Can't Be Done; Gibraltar Anthem (Willey/Bridges); Safe In My Arms; Didn't We (Webb); Say It With Flowers; *Medley*: This Is My Mother's Day/A Tree In The Meadow/I'm Walking Behind You; I Can Live Again; I've Gotta Be Me

1972
President PT374 If He Walked Into My Life (Herman)
Let Me Take Care Of You (Squires)

President PTLS1049/50 Double LP *Dorothy Squires At The London Palladium December 5th 1971*
Happy Heart (Last/Rae); There Goes My Heart (Davis/ Silver); Shaking The Blues Away (Berlin); Where Do I Begin (Lai/Sigman); Bewitched (Rodgers/Hart); *Autograph Book*: What A Wonderful World (Weiss/Douglas)/As Long As He Needs Me (Bart)/Mother Kelly's Doorstep (Stevens) /Mother's Day; Everything's Coming Up Roses (Sondheim/ Styne); My Way; Life Goes On; For Once In My Life; If He Walked Into My Life (Herman); *The Irony of War Medley*: Where Have All The Flowers Gone (Seeger)/When The World Is Ready (Scott/Black)/Glory Hallelujah (Traditional)/ Pack Up Your Troubles In Your Old Kit Bag(Powell/Asaf)/ Goodbye Dolly Gray (Barnes/Cobb)/It's A Long Way To Tipperary (Williams/ Judge)/Maman (Thomas/Charnin); When There's Love In Your Heart; I've Gotta Be Me

Bell 282 If I Could Go Back
　　　　　As The Saying Goes (Squires)

Starline SRS55114 LP *The Essential Dorothy Squires*
Say It With Flowers; Roses Of Picardy; Moonlight And Roses; Unforgettable; The Gypsy; I'll Close My Eyes; I Remember The Cornfields; I'm In The Mood For Love; Be My Love; A Tree In The Meadow; Anytime; Once In A While; Faith; At The End Of The Day; Mistakes; How Deep Is The Ocean (compilation)

1973
Pye NSPL18425 LP *Cheese 'N' Wine* (with Dennis Lotis)
Cheese And Wine (Squires); I Never Thought (Squires) I'd Like To Make It With You (Gates); Speak Softly To Me (Coleman); In The Still Of The Night (Porter); And I Love You So (McLean); Take Me (Bloom/David); If Ever I Would Leave You (Lerner/Loew); It's Impossible (Manzero/ Wayne); Softly As I Leave You (Calabrese/DeVita/Shaper); Always (Berlin); Cheese And Wine

BBC: ND *Dorothy Squires: Star For A Week*
Roses Of Picardy; Moonlight And Roses; I'll Be With You
In Apple Blossom Time; Your Flowers Arrived Too Late;
Tulips From Amsterdam; When The Poppies Bloom Again;
We'll Gather Lilacs; Say It With Flowers; Without You;
You'll Never Walk Alone; At The End Of The Day;
Solitude's My Home; If I Could Go Back; My Way. Live
recording with the BBC Northern Dance Orchestra.
Unreleased.

EMI EMC3004 LP *Dorothy Again! Dorothy Squires At
The London Palladium 26 November 1972*
I Only Wanna Laugh (Jacob); I Wish You Love; Without
You(Ham/Evans); *Flowers Medley*: Roses Of Picardy/
Moonlight And Roses/I'll Be With You In Apple Blossom
Time/Your Flowers Arrived Too Late/Tulips From
Amsterdam/When The Poppies Bloom Again/We'll Gather
Lilacs/Say It With Flowers; Stardust (Carmichael/Parish);
You'll Never Walk Alone; When You Lose The One You
Love; If (Gates); Solitude's My Home; Tammy Tell Me
True; If I Could Go Back (Bacharach/David); With All My
Heart

Pye ??? Don't Take Your Love From Me (released 1999)

EMI 2039   Solitude's My Home (Ma solitude)
            (Moustaki/McKuen
              How Deep Is The Ocean (Berlin)

1974

Pye NSPD501 Double LP *Dorothy Squires Live At The Theatre Royal, Drury Lane*
Heck Of A Score (Squires);Open A New Window (Herman)
My Best Girl (with Michael Ward); *Mame Medley*: If He
Walked Into My Life/Open A New Window/Mame (Herman)
Some People Are Born (Squires)/Nobody Does It Like Me*
(Coleman/Fields); Raindrops Keep Falling On My Head
(Bacharach/David); Who Else But Me (Brown); Smile
(Chaplin/Turner/Parsons); Something Greater; I'm Walking
Behind You; On The Sunny Side Of The Street (McHugh/
Fields); Danny Boy (Weatherly/Samuel); Young Men With
Heads On High (Squires); Whippenpoof Song (Samuels/
Minnegerode/Pomeroy);Until The Real Thing Comes Along
(Cahn/Holiner/Chaplin/Freeman); Eyes Of A Man; Some
Enchanted Evening (Rodgers/Hammerstein); Hello, Young
Lovers (Rodgers/Hammerstein); I Could Have Danced All
Night (Lerner/Loew); Will There Be A Place (Squires/Eden/
Dunstall); Heart Of A City (Squires/Eden/Dunstall); Climb
Every Mountain (Rodgers/Hammerstein); Going Nowhere
(Holland) *The album was recalled after complaints from
the composers and re-released minus this song.

Pye 7N45384 Something Greater (Strauss/Adams)
Find A Way Back (Squires/Dunstall)

Pye ??? The Eyes Of The Beholder (Squires) Unreleased

1975
Pye 7N45446 The Impossible Dream (Leigh/Darion
Eyes Of A Man (Squires/Dunstall)

Pye ??? This Is All I Ask (Jenkins) Released in 1999

Pye ??? Maybe This Time (Kander/Ebb) Released in 1999.

1977

Decca TXS122   LP **Rain, Rain, Go Away**
We Clowns; Born To Lose (Bardotto/Bembo/Newell);
Megan (Squires/Newell); I'll Close My Eyes; It Can't Be
Wrong (Steiner/Gannon); If I Never Sing Another Song
(Alexandra/Jurgens/Black); Here's That Rainy Day (Burke/
Van Heusen); Passing Strangers; Love Letters (Herman/
Young); The Way We Were (Hamlisch/Bergman/Bergman)
Is That All There Is (Leiber/Stoller); If I Had A Chance

Decca F13720 If I Had A Chance (Squires)
              Passing Strangers (Mitchell/Mann)

President PT490 We Clowns (Squires)
              I'm Glad There Is You (Mertz/Dorsey)

Pye GH639 LP   **Golden Hour Presents Dorothy Squires**
The Gypsy; Open A New Window; I'll Close My Eyes;
Cheese And Wine; Yes I'll Be Here; Mother's Day; *Mame
Medley*: If He Walked Into My Life/Open A New Window/
Mame; Raindrops Keep Falling On My Head; I'm Walking
Behind You; Danny Boy; In All The World; It's A Pity To
Say Goodnight; Climb Every Mountain; My Way (Instr);
Going Nowhere (compilation)

1979

ESBAN LP *Old Rowley: The Musical* (unreleased)
Pudding; Old Rowley; By Royal Command; Will There Be
A Place; A Friend Is Someone; Heart of the City; My
Room; Sleep, Sleep, My Baby; Can't Put A Price On Love;
Doth Thou Love Me Nell; You Waken One Morning; The
King Is Dead; Finale: Old Rowley Medley. A concept
devised by Dorothy, written/composed by her, Mark Eden
and Ernie Dunstall. Recorded at the Dominion Theatre.

Decca DPA3073/4 Double LP *With All My Heart*
The Gypsy; It's A Pity To Say Goodnight; When You Lose
The One You Love; I'll Close My Eyes; Changing Partners;
Danger Ahead; Don't Search For Love; White Wings; With
All My Heart; When I Grow Too Old To Dream; Yes, I'll Be
There; Torremolinos;A Tree In The Meadow; I Still Believe;
In All The World; Come Home To My Arms; Safe In My
Arms; Sorrento And You; Mother's Day; Coming Home; I'm
Walking Behind You; Someone To Love; Blue, Blue, Blue;
Reflections In The Water (compilation).

1980

ESBAN 001 LP *We Clowns: Live At The Dominion Theatre*
A Lovely Way To Spend An Evening (McHugh/Adamson); Can't Smile Without You (Arnold/Martin/Morrow); Close Your Eyes, I'll Stay Beside You (Squires); Help Me Make It Through The Night (Kristofferson); Never, Never, Never (Renis/Testa/Newell); New York New York (Kander/Webb); You'll Never Walk Alone (Rodgers/Hammerstein); May You Always (Marke/Charles); I'm Glad There Is You (Madeira/Dorsey); We Clowns; *Hit Medley*: Say It With Flowers/For Once In My Life/Till/My Way. ("I Remember It Well" was removed from the second printing of the LP.

ESBAN Feelings (Albert/Gatse) (Recorded at the Dominion Theatre, later released by President)

1983
Pye (unknown) LP *May You Always*
May You Always; New York, New York; We Clowns; Can't Smile Without You; A Lovely Way To Spend An Evening; I'm Glad There Is You; Feelings; Will There Be A Place; Open A New Window; Heart Of The City; Close Your Eyes, I'll Stay Beside You/Help Me Make It Through The Night *
        *These songs were recorded, but the album aborted

The Chosen One (Squires/Brown) released 1999.

1984
Esban ES9 I Am What I Am (Herman)*
　　　　　Legend In My Time (Gibson) recorded 12/83.

Esban ES10 You'll Never Walk Alone
　　　　　I'm Glad There Is You

I Wear My Heart Upon My Sleeve (Berliner/Bret)*
Solitude (Barbara/Bret)*
The Unknown Town (Dumont/Bret)*
　　*Tape recordings)

Conifer CFRC521 LP ***Three Beautiful Words of Love***
The Gypsy; Let The Rest Of The World Go By; Memories Of You; Three Beautiful Words Of Love; I Love You For Sentimental Reasons; Danger Ahead; Laughing On The Outside, Crying On The Inside; It's A Pity To Say Goodnight; My First Love, My Last Love For Always; On The Sunny Side Of The Street; Do I Worry; Baby Come Home; Yes, I'll Be Here; Bewitched; Talk It Over With Someone; Say It With Flowers (compilation)

1987
Esban ES14 The Wine Is There (Squires) with Darren Wells
　　　　　Try A Little Tenderness (Woods/Campbell/Connelly)

Appendix 2
Songs Written by Dorothy Squires

Items marked * have no dates.

Acapulco Mexico *
Are you? (1962)
As Long As You Love Me*
As The Saying Goes (1972)
Blue Skies *
Bord Na Mona *
Call Of Spring, The (1966)
Charmeuse *
Chez Moi *
Cheese And Wine (1974)
Chosen One, The (1983)
Clackers *
Close Your Eyes, I'll Stay Beside You (1979)
Come Home To My Arms (1956)
Don't Ask Me Why (1971)
Don't Search For Love (1957)
Esther (with Roger Moore) *
Eventide (with Ernie Dunstall) (1955)
Eyes Of A Man (with Ernie Dunstall) (1974)
Eyes Of The Beholder (1974)
Find A Way Back (with Ernie Dunstall) (1974)

For Emily *
Gaiety High *
Goodbye (with Ernie Dunstall) (1966)
Good Things*
Guiding Hand*
Half A Chance*
Handle With Care*
Happy To Know
Have I Waited Too Long (with Ernie Dunstall) (1966)
Heart Of A City*
Heck Of A Score*
I Can Live Again (1970)
If I Had A Chance (1974)
I'll Come A Running*
I Love The Queen*
I Love You*
I Never Thought
It Can't Be Done (1970)
I Won't Cry Anymore (with Ernie Dunstall) (1963)
Lay Day*
Legend Of The Well (1952)
Let Me Take Care Of You (1971)
Letting Go*
Lisa's Song
Look Around (with Ernie Dunstall) (1964)
Maid Of The Valley (1953)
Man Says*
Megan's Theme (1977)
Never Let Him Know*
Nice To See You*
Nos Da*
Old Rowley*
Once Upon A Time (1963)
One More Chance*
Opening Song*
Our Garden (1968)
Our Song (1957)

Plane Jane*
Play It To The Rules (1968)
Point Of No Return (1968)
Red The Rose (1963)
Sapphic Dream*
Say It With Flowers (1961)
Seasons Of (1968)
Secret Diary*
Secret That's Never Been Told, A (with Ernie Dunstall) (1957)
Set Me Free (with Ernie Dunstall) (1955)
She's That Someone (1973)
Sneaking Up*
Someone Other Than Me (with Ernie Dunstall) (1966)
Some People Are Born*
Spillover*
Sticks And Stones (1956)
Tammy, Tell Me True (1961)
Theme For David*
There's No Room In My Heart*
Things To Do In My Life*
This Place Called Home*
Time*
Torremolinos (1956)
Two Strangers Met (with Ernie Dunstall) (1964)
Waken Up One Morning*
We Clowns (1977)
What Is The Reason?*
What'll I Do?*
When There's Love In Your Heart (1968)
Where Can I Go? (1968)
Will There Be A Place? (1972)
Whoever (1962)
Wine Is There, The (1984)
Wish*
You Can Tell*

Appendix III
Filmography

WIT AND WISDOM (1948) BBC TV Movie, 45 mins.
Producer: Richard Afton. Music: Eric Robinson, With Norman Wisdom, Billy Reid and the Arnott Brothers. No other details.

STARS IN THEIR EYES (1956) Grand Alliance/British Lion Films, 96 mins.

Director: Maurice Elvey. Script: Maurice Elvey/Jack Hulbert, based on a story by Francis Miller. Photography: S D Onions. Costumes: Laura Nightingale. With Pat Kirkwood, Nat Jackley, Bonar Colleano, Vera Day, Hubert Gregg, Jimmie Clitheroe. Dorothy (3rd billing) played Ann Hart. Songs: "Has Anybody Here Seen Kelly ?" (Murphy/Letters) *, "Stars In My Eyes" (Gregg) *, "I Saw The Look In Your Eyes" **, "The Man That Wakes The Man That Blows Reveille" (Gregg)*, "I'd Pick Piccadilly" (Gregg) *, "Without You" (Astley/Elms/Harvey" *, "A Man And His Music" (Gregg)***, "With All My Heart" ****, "My Boy" (Pelosi/Towers) *****
*sung by Pat Kirkwood, **sung by Dorothy and Colleano (separately), ***sung by Nat Jackley, ****sung by Dorothy and Bonar Colleano, ***** sung by Jackley and Jimmy Clitheroe.

"Watch it, boyo!"

Source Notes & Bibliography

Billboard: "Squires Concert Is Good Investment", 11/72; "Kassner Appears For UK Payola Probe", 6/73.

BENSON, Ross: Dorothy's Sad Plea To Moore", *Daily Express*, 3/95; "Squires' Gypsy Life Turns Full Circle", *Daily Express*, 5/95.

BRET, David: Interviews with Marion Montgomery, Nicky Welsh, Johnnie Gray, "Tom", Kenny Brown; *Diana Dors: Hurricane In Mink*, JR Books, 2010; *Brit Girls of the Sixties: Dusty Springfield & Helen Shapiro*, DbBooks, 2012.

CABLE, Michael: "Dorothy Squires: Americans Are Bastards To British Artists", *Easy Listening*, 5/73.

CROFT, Charles: "Dorothy, The Racing Owner Who Says It With Kisses", *The Star*, 12/75.

COURCY, Anne de: "Destroyed By Her Love For Roger Moore", *Daily Mail*, 4/98.

DAVIES, Jessica: "The Star Who Loved And Lost: Why Dorothy Squires Will Never Forgive Roger Moore", *Daily Mail*, 8/94.

DORS, Diana: *Behind Closed Doors*, W H Allen, 1979.

DOW, Mike: "Mike Dow Talks To Dorothy Squires", OUT, 12/84.

DRAKE, Michael: "Legend Lotis Bows Out In Style", *Eastern Daily Press* (Norfolk), 8/05.

EDEN, Mark: *Who's Going To Look At You?* Troubadour, 2010.

FRANKLIN, Joe & STOKES, Alison: "Singing Legend Dorothy Dies", *South Wales Echo*, 4/98.

GLENTON, George: "My One Regret By Dorothy Squires", *Daily Mirror*, 1974.

GRACIE, Charlie (with John J Jackson): *Rock & Roll's Hidden Giant*, Alfred Publishing, 2014.

GREENSMITH, Jim: "Dynamic Dot, Who Started In Sheffield At £5 A Week", *Sheffield Star*, 9/72.

HICKEY, William: "Uneasy Peace As Dot Is Laid To Rest", *Daily Mail*, 1998.

JONES, Janie: *The Devil & Miss Jones*, Smith Gryphon, 1993.

KEMPSON, Trevor, COOKE, Clive and others: "The Payola Scandal", *News of the World*, 2/3/4/1971.

MATTIOLI, Luisa: "Roger Moore & His Wife: He's The New James Bond", syndicated US feature, 1/73.

MOORE, Roger: *My Word Is My Bond*, O'Mara, 2008.

Moore Vs News of the World: Case Ref: 1-QB-44 (1972)

NEILL, Sir Brian, QC: *The Neill Report* (Payola) 1971.

NEWNHAM, John K: "The Marriage They Said Couldn't Last", *TV Mirror*, 3/58.

NEWLEY, Patrick: "Dorothy Come Home", *The Stage*, 11/94; "Remembering Dorothy Squires", *The* Stage, 5/98.

"PARISS": "Dorothy Squires": *QX*, 1998.

PITMAN, Jenny: *Jenny Pitman: The Autobiography.*

PRIDE, Margaret: "The Courage of Dorothy Squires", *Reveille*, 1973.

ROBBINS, Christopher: *The Empress of Ireland*, Simon & Schuster, 2005.

ROBERTS, Glenys: "Roger Moore", *Daily Mail*, 9/12.

ROGERS, Linda: "Dot And Her Two-Fingered Exit", *Chatham Daily News*, 1974.

SQUIRES, Dorothy: Interviews & Conversations with David Bret, 1972-97; Interview with *Radio Pictorial*, undated; *Rain, Rain Go Away*, unpublished memoirs, 1977; Interview with Harlech Television, 1977; Interview with Ed Moreno, RNI, 2/71; *Rain, Rain Go Away: The Dorothy Squires Story*, BBC Wales, 1998.

STEWART, Tony: "Dot, Pot & Growing Old Gracefully", *New Musical Express*, 1974.

Various: "Who Is Charlie Grace, Anyway?" *Daily Sketch, London Chronicle* and other publications, 8/57.

WILDER, Rosalyn: "Dorothy Squires: Talk of The Town", *Call Boy*, Autumn 2011.

Zec, Donald: "My Night Out At The Cat Fight", *Sunday Mirror*, 3/76.

ANONYMOUS: "Sandra Dee", *Daily Mail*, 2/05; "Revealed, Heath's Secret Harmony With Star Squires", *Daily Express*, 7/05; "Crooner On The Air: Young Llanellyite To Broadcast",*Llanelli & County Guardian*, 2/36; "Dorothy Brings Drury Lane Premiere To Cabaret Candlelight", *Llanelli Star*, 10/73.

Win a family holiday in Mee... Florida and DisneyWorld ...st

Start collecting tokens in tomorrow's Echo

SINGING LEGEND DOROTHY DIES

SINGER Dorothy Squires died today after a long battle against cancer.

The Llanelli-born, 83-year-old former wife of James Bond star Roger Moore died from lung cancer just a year after being given the all-clear by doctors.

The 1950s star, real name Edna May Moore, died at Llwynypia Hospital, Rhondda, at 2.05am, where she had been since March following a fall.

She died peacefully after a telephone call from her former husband, 13 years her junior, who she never stopped loving.

Her close friend, royal biographer Michael Thornton, said "She died peacefully and at peace with the world.

"She knew she was dying, but never lost her fighting spirit or her extraordinary courage.

"She was still smiling and joking to the very end. Roger Moore rang

By Jo Franklin and Alison Stokes

the hospital last night and told Dorothy's niece, Emily-Jane Squires. Take hold of her hand, give it a little squeeze and tell her Rog is thinking of her'.

"When she was given Roger's message, Dorothy smiled and spoke just one word: 'Magic'," he said.

Mr Thornton said Mr Moore had been told of her death.

Arrangements are being made by Ms Squire's niece, Emily-Jane, for two services to be held – one in Port Talbot and one in London.

The singing sensation will be buried with her parents in London's Streatham Park cemetery.

Ms Squires married Roger Moore in 1953 when he was an unknown 25-year-old actor.

But he walked out on

her in 1961 for 28-year-old Italian actress Luisa Mattioli, who was the leading lady in his latest film.

Ms Squire's fame dwindled, she became bankrupt and was evicted from her Berkshire home.

She lived as a recluse in a £180,000 Trebanog house, given to her rent-free by dedicated fan Fame Coles, for three years until her fall in February.

In 1996 she had a bladder tumour removed.

Although she had been given the all-clear, doctors at East Glamorgan Hospital, Church Village, who were treating Ms Squires after her fall, discovered the cancer had spread to her lungs.

She was later transferred to Llwynypia Hospital, where she died.

■ Life went full circle for star Dorothy – obituary. See Page 4

► STAR COUPLE *International star Dorothy Squires, above, in her heyday and, left, with Roger Moore. The couple married in 1953.*

237

In Loving Memory
of
Dorothy Squires

Service at
St. Mary's Church
Port Talbot
on
Tuesday 21st April 1998
at 2:00 p.m.
and at Streatham Park Cemetery
on
Friday 24th April 1998
at 1:00 p.m.
Followed by Interment in the Cemetery

Acknowledgements

Writing this book would not have been possible had it not been for the inspiration, criticisms and love of that select group of individuals who, whether they be in this world or the next, I will always regard as my true family and *autre coeur*: Barbara, Irene Bevan, Marlene Dietrich, René and Lucette Chevalier, Axel Dotti, Anne Taylor and Roger Normand, David Bolt, *que vous dormez en paix*, Jacqueline Danno, Russ Conway, Hélène Delavault, Betty and Gérard Gamain, Annick Roux, Terry Sanderson, Charley Marouani, Doris Gaard, Simon Blumenfeld, Hilda Brown, Johnnie Gray, Nicky Welsh, Chris Rogers, Holly Wendland, Pat Kirkwood, Marion Montgomery. Also a very special mention for Amália Rodrigues, Peter Burton, Joey Stefano, those *hiboux, fadistas* and *amis de foutre* who happened along the way, and *mes enfants perdus*. Thanks too to my wife, Jeanne, for putting up with my bad moods and for still being the keeper of my soul!

And a big, BIG hug for Dot, for being there!